Innovations in Education Series
Edited by Robert J. Brown

1. Edward J. Dirkswager, editor. *Teachers as Owners: A Key to Revitalizing Public Education.* 2002.
2. Darlene Leiding. *The Won't Learners: An Answer to Their Cry.* 2002.
3. Ronald J. Newell. *Passion for Learning: How a Project-Based System Meets the Needs of High School Students in the 21st Century.* 2003.
4. Sarah J. Noonan. *The Elements of Leadership: What You Should Know.* 2003.
5. Jeffrey R. Cornwall. *From the Ground Up: Entrepreneurial School Leadership.* 2003.
6. Linda Schaak Distad and Joan Cady Brownstein. *Talking Teaching: Implementing Reflective Practice in Groups.* 2004.

Talking Teaching

Implementing Reflective Practice in Groups

Linda Schaak Distad
Joan Cady Brownstein

Innovations in Education, No. 6

ScarecrowEducation
Lanham, Maryland • Toronto • Oxford
2004

Published in the United States of America
by ScarecrowEducation
An imprint of The Rowman & Littlefield Publishing Group, Inc.
4501 Forbes Boulevard, Suite 200, Lanham, Maryland 20706
www.scarecroweducation.com

PO Box 317
Oxford
OX2 9RU, UK

British Library Cataloguing in Publication Information Available

Library of Congress Cataloging-in-Publication Data

Distad, Linda Schaak, 1949–
  Talking teaching : implementing reflective practice in groups / Linda
Schaak Distad, Joan Cady Brownstein.
    p. cm. — (Innovations in education ; no. 6)
  Includes bibliographical references and index.
  ISBN 1-57886-090-3 (pbk. : alk. paper)
  1. Reflective teaching. 2. Group work in education. I. Brownstein,
Joan Cady, 1943– II. Title. III. Series: Innovations in education
(Lanham, Md.) ; no. 6.
LB1027 .D539 2004
371.39'5—dc22
                                          2003021728

To Dick, Liz, Tom, and Mike
　　　　　　—L. S. D.

To Jack
　　　　—J. C. B.

Contents

List of Figures and Tables

FIGURES

TABLES

Preface

Sitting in her Reflective Practice Group, the beginning teacher, with tears streaming down her face, told her story.

> I really looked forward to my first teaching job. I worked hard to get my teaching license and I was excited to begin, but it's so hard. I have to go to several buildings. I eat lunch in my car on the way between buildings. There's no time in the day to write up the reports I'm required by law to file on my special needs kids. I don't feel connected to any building because I rarely have time to talk to any of the other teachers. When I get home at night, it's more work to stay caught up. I don't get to exercise anymore. I used to jog every day. My husband is mad because we never get to talk together; he says he doesn't know who I am anymore. I'm tired all of the time and I feel like I'm coming apart at the seams.

Many teachers enter the profession with next to no support in their beginning years. They work in isolation with little opportunity to interact with colleagues. They are left to problem solve and gain experiential knowledge by trial and error. This approach works for some but also causes nearly one-third of all teachers (and almost half of urban teachers) to quit teaching in the first five years.[1]

Through the process of writing this book, we have had the time to consider the significance of our experiences with Reflective Practice Groups (RPGs) in a three-year teacher induction program with a suburban school district. We experienced the emotional tone of meetings, the exuberance of group members to offer advice in response to a participant's critical incident, and their hesitancy to discuss theory.

Teaching requires experience and knowledge for the development of one's repertoire of strategies and techniques for dealing with the unexpected. Novice teachers especially need support and advice during the first years of teaching: what to do when lessons do not go as planned, when students are not motivated or challenged, when parents are demanding, when colleagues are nonsupportive, or when public and governmental criticism of the profession abounds.

The initial wave of "practical tools and emotional supports" should not be the end or the only assistance provided new teachers. Reading, discussing, and applying theory to classroom problems are essential activities for teacher growth and development. When teachers own the purpose and understand a new practice, they are more likely to use it successfully in their teaching. RPGs provide the opportunity to process, clarify, and expand personal beliefs and understandings about teaching.

NOTES

1. National Commission on Teaching and America's Future, *No Dream Denied*. 2003 (www.ndtaf.org).

Acknowledgments

We would like to thank the following persons: Richard Germundsen, Betsy Chase, Margaret Reif, Julie Robbins, education faculty from the Associated Colleges of the Twin Cities, teachers and administrators from our reflective practice groups, and students from the College of St. Catherine and the University of St. Thomas.

CHAPTER 1

What Are Reflective Practice Groups?

Think back to your first days as a teacher. What kind of support did you receive from your district? If you have taught for fewer than ten years, you may have been assigned a building mentor or you were required to attend "skills sessions" that focused on developing specific strategies. If you have taught for more than ten years, you probably had an experience similar to ours.

First, we remember the thrill of being hired during a time when jobs were tight. Next, we remember the excitement of going to our classrooms for the first time, looking at the student work areas, and examining the bulletin boards and shelves of materials. Then came the panic—"I'm the teacher! I don't know how to teach! I don't know what to teach!" But, like all the other new teachers in our districts, we struggled through the first year afraid to let on to our colleagues that we needed help. Although we made it, not everyone did. We can all cite examples of teachers who left the profession during their first years. Alone and overwhelmed, some simply could not deal with the constant barrage of challenges that life in the classroom represents. No wonder so many new teachers did not persist long enough to become tenured.

Thirty years later, the atmosphere for new teachers is not much better. Faced with increasingly complex teaching challenges, new teachers are easily overwhelmed by the pressures and pulls of life in the classroom. Without frequent, nonevaluative support, the probability of success is greatly diminished. With this in mind, we developed a Reflective Practice Group (RPG) process to use with teachers.

When we talk about RPGs, we are describing a particular *way for teachers to regularly and systematically reflect on their practice in a supportive, collegial environment free from evaluation*. Teachers need to talk freely about professional concerns with their colleagues without fearing that the information will be used against them in an evaluation process or a contract decision. Trust and confidentiality are critical elements of the Reflective Practice Group process.

Reflection is part of professional behavior. If there is any doubt about this, simply check the most prominent current educational research. For example, in Charlotte Danielson's *Framework: Domain Four*, she identifies "reflecting on teaching" as a component of a teacher's professional responsibilities.[1] Similarly, *Praxis III: Domain Four* discusses "Reflecting on Teaching."[2] Two of the five core propositions of the National Board for Professional Teaching Standards address areas of reflective practice. Core Proposition Four states that "Teachers think systematically about their practice and learn from experience." Core Proposition Five says, "Teachers are members of learning communities."[3] Reflective practice combines these elements by creating learning communities in which teachers gather to examine their practice.

Our work with RPGs began in 1996 when the Minnesota Board of Teaching funded seven pilot projects that investigated a variety of approaches for supporting first-year teachers. Our project brought beginning teachers and teachers new to the school district together with experienced teachers and teacher educators to reflect regularly and systematically on instruction and classroom issues.

The district was in a rapidly growing suburban area just outside the Twin Cities of St. Paul and Minneapolis, Minnesota. The district's beginning teachers had expressed the need to talk about teaching challenges with other teachers. Through our work at our colleges, we had experience working with teaching triads and other methods of reflective practice, so we agreed to design and implement Reflective Practice Groups as a component of the induction year activities. One of the professors suggested a Freirian model, which surfaced through a Fulbright Scholar exchange in Chile and had been studied in faculty and student teacher applications.[4] Over the years, the original ten-step process was refined into an eight-step process. We also drew heavily from the work of John Dewey.

John Dewey helps us understand why reflection is such an important component of professional behavior. He defines reflective thought as a process in which the basics for beliefs are examined. He explained that reflection "involves not simply a sequence of ideas, but a consequence— a consecutive ordering in such a way that each determines the next as its proper outcome, while each in turn leans back on its predecessors."[5] RPGs use a structured, sequential process to deconstruct, analyze, and interpret critical professional events. Participants share challenging teaching situations via an eight-step process.

This book presents our RPG process and experiences. Ten interactive case studies are also included for the reader to work through the process and consider his or her own connections between teaching beliefs and teaching practices.

What are the traditions of reflective practice groups? We look at these traditions in the next chapter.

NOTES

1. Charlotte Danielson, *Enhancing Professional Practice: A Framework for Teachers* (Alexandria, Va.: Association for Supervision and Curriculum Development, 1996).

2. Educational Testing Service, *Praxis III: Classroom Performance Assessments* (www.ets.org).

3. National Board for Professional Teaching Standards (www.nbpts.org).

4. G. R. Vera, *Methodologias de Investigaction Docente: La Investigacion Protagonica* (Santiago, Chile: Programa Interdisciplinario de Investigacion en Educacion, 1988).

5. John Dewey, *How We Think* (New York: Dover Publications, 1920/1997), 2.

CHAPTER 2

The Tradition of Reflective Practice Groups

The concept of teachers discussing their teaching and curriculum is not a new phenomenon. For example, teacher discussion groups were held regularly in the Dewey Laboratory School at the University of Chicago at the turn of the twentieth century. At the Dewey School, "Intellectual freedom to think and act on one's thoughts and ideals" was essential for teachers.[1] Teachers participated in the development of curriculum and instruction along with all members of the school community. Laurel Tanner suggests that if we want to improve teaching and curriculum, we look to "seminar-type discussions where problems are considered in their theoretical as well as practical relations."[2] At the Dewey School, teachers submitted weekly reports that addressed what was taught and why. They also met in weekly seminars to discuss their work and attend classes. Although influential in the progressive era, the lessons learned at the Dewey Lab School were largely lost in subsequent years.

In the 1980s and 1990s, however, the idea of teacher reflection returned with great enthusiasm. Donald Schön introduced the concept of the "reflective practitioner" as the role of the teacher making decisions before and after teaching ("reflection-on-action") and decisions during lessons ("reflection-in-action").[3] Brookfield introduces the concept of the "critically reflective teacher." He suggests that the purposes of critical reflection are to understand the influence of power in education and "to question assumptions and practices."[4] When talking with our colleagues, Brookfield asks teachers to share "critical incidents" or "high and low moments in their practice, or details of significant incidents that stand out in their lives as teachers."[5]

Parker Palmer also supports the value of group reflection or "the conversation of colleagues" for improving teaching. He suggests that the conversations be framed around the "critical moments" of teaching when "a learning opportunity for students will open up, or shut down—depending, in part, on how the teacher handles it."[6]

Currently, reflecting in groups may include "dialogue, study, or support groups; action research groups; group discussion of a course syllabus, lesson plan, or teaching strategy; or on-line chat groups."[7] College faculty engage in reflective practice through "teaching and learning seminars, brown-bag lunch discussions, teaching circles, connected teaching strategies, and reflective practice groups."[8] Countries outside of the United States also use reflective practice groups, such as networking new teachers in New Zealand and group lesson study and observation in Japan.[9]

Clearly, reflective practice has value, but why? What are the benefits of reflective practice? We examine these benefits in the next chapter.

NOTES

1. Laurel Tanner, *Dewey's Laboratory School: Lessons for Today* (New York: Teachers College Press, 1997), 112.

2. Tanner: 168.

3. Donald Schön, *The Reflective Practitioner: How Professionals Think in Action* (New York: Basic Books, 1983).

4. Stephen D. Brookfield, *Becoming a Critically Reflective Teacher* (San Francisco: Jossey-Bass, 1995), 3.

5. Brookfield: 47–8.

6. Parker J. Palmer, *The Courage to Teach: Exploring the Inner Landscape of a Teacher's Life* (San Francisco: Jossey-Bass, 1998), 145.

7. A Project of the Institute on Disability, UAP, University of New Hampshire, "Teaching and Learning Tools: What Is Reflective Practice?" (http://iod.unh.edu/EE/archive-reflective.html), 1.

8. Center for Instructional Development and Research, "Talking with Colleagues about Teaching-Resources and Examples" (http://depts.Washington.edu/cidrweb/conversations.html), 1

9. Kendyll Stansbury and Joy Zimmerman, *Lifelines to the Classroom: Designing Support for Beginning Teachers* (San Francisco: WestEd, 2000), 11.

CHAPTER 3

Empowering Teachers
through Reflective Practice

What happens when teachers reflect with each other about their practice? In using Reflective Practice Groups (RPGs), Chase, Germundsen, Cady Brownstein, and Distad report that teachers' confidence increases; their repertoire of problem-solving skills increases; and their overall sense of professional efficacy increases.[1] As shown in Figure 3.1, we connect RPGs and higher teacher efficacy, which in turn leads to increased student learning.

To begin this discussion, a couple of reminders about terminology might be helpful. *Reflective Practice Groups* refers to a very specific process in which teachers are provided a way to regularly and systematically reflect on their practice in a supportive, collegial environment free from evaluation. Confidentiality and adherence to the eight-step process are essential for RPGs' success.

The next term we need to define is *efficacy.* Efficacy describes a teacher's belief that he or she has the skills necessary to effect positive changes in student learning. Teachers with a strong sense of efficacy feel more confident, affirmed, and validated by their experiences in the classroom. Their language about teaching is hopeful and positive.

Teachers with high efficacy have a large repertoire of teaching skills. This is important because one teaching situation may require multiple approaches. A teacher with a large repertoire does not feel defeated when the first or only strategy does not work. She is prepared with another plan or additional approaches to the problem. She understands the subtleties of a situation. She may even feel exhilarated by the challenges of the profession. However, when a strategy does not work, a teacher

Reflective Practice Groups

↓

High Teacher Efficacy

↓

Increased Student Learning!

Figure 3.1.   *Reflective Practice Groups and Student Learning*

with low efficacy takes this as a personal professional affront. Over time, low efficacy teachers become discouraged and leave the profession, either literally or figuratively.

Teachers with high efficacy regularly reflect on teaching. The RPGs use a structured, sequential process to deconstruct, analyze, and interpret critical professional events. Plus, some of the barriers usually associated with asking advice from colleagues are eliminated. Because the conversations within the groups are completely confidential, group members receive candid feedback without the fear of reprisal or apprehension that the information might be included in a performance review. Reflection must not just look back. As shown in Figure 3.2, reflecting back coupled with forward thinking, creates a process for learning from one's experiences.

Teachers with a strong sense of efficacy believe they are skilled at managing and organizing a classroom. They also recognize that organization and classroom management should not be left to chance. Both are highly sophisticated skills that effective teachers employ to create a productive learning environment in their classrooms.

Table 3.1 reveals the response of participants during the three years we worked with RPGs in one district.

As for all teachers, classroom management and student behavior were of continuing concern to the RPG participants. They found that the systematic reflective sharing helped them to increase their ability to

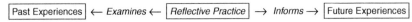

Past Experiences ← *Examines* ← *Reflective Practice* → *Informs* → Future Experiences

Figure 3.2.   *Reflective Practice Groups: Understanding Past and Future*

Table 3.1. *Data from Reflective Practice Groups*

	Beginning Teachers	Experienced Teachers
Did you gain any insights from your colleague in the RPGs?	100%	95%
Did the RPG help you to improve as a teacher?	73%	63%

create more positive environments in the classroom. Here are some of their comments:

> "I learned of a few discipline tricks that helped settle my class down."
> "I've learned to hold students more accountable for their actions as well as create clearer expectations and consequences, not rules and punishments."
> "I think student performance has improved because of my attendance at RPG meetings. My class is more organized."
> "In a couple of specific cases I have seen struggling students become much more focused and improve their habits."

This language indicates the increasing efficacy of teachers. They recognize that they have the power to positively impact student learning. They attribute their increased knowledge to their involvement with colleagues in a reflective process.

In addition to classroom management and organization, a large number of teachers spoke of increased satisfaction, affirmation, validation, and confidence. Teachers repeatedly made comments indicating that they believed their ability to problem solve had improved; they viewed challenges as energizing rather than defeating. Most importantly, though, they started to make the connection between their improved efficacy and increased student learning. A few of their comments demonstrate this:

> "I believe I have become more confident as a teacher and I am able to tap into my building's resources because of this group and the knowledge I have gained this first year."
> "I think that my students have benefited from RPGs because I feel more supported in the actions I take."
> "Student performance was improved because I became more confident."

"When a person is happy and feeling positive about their job and colleagues (support, warmth) they are able to really concentrate on their jobs and students. Also . . . we can be open and thrive in a safe, supportive, and structured environment, so too, students need this to be successful and happy at school."

A third area that many teachers mentioned included an increased repertoire of teaching skills. According to participants, this sense of professional efficacy or power positively impacted student learning. The following are some of their comments:

"I have used some of the strategies we discussed in our RPGs and I feel they have helped my classroom atmosphere and teaching, e.g., attendance policies, discipline issues, parent-teacher conferences, and curriculum writing."

"I find myself teaming more and asking for the perspectives of others and ultimately this pays off in improved student performance and to the collaborative efforts."

"Student performance has improved because I am a more effective teacher. It is easier for me to make my points because I am prepared for possible actions by my students. I have been able to use more techniques that I have learned through the RPG to raise student achievement."

The final group of responses from teachers about their experiences with RPGs referred to becoming more reflective. Many teachers used terminology that included "stepping back" and gaining new perspectives.

"I feel that I have taken the time to step back and look at what I am doing as an educator and make some positive adjustments. It has helped give me a fresh perspective on my classroom."

"I liked how I could stand back and look at the student behavior and actions in class . . . how to self-evaluate my lessons, discipline and consequences."

"Generally, it has helped me to perhaps step back and take a fresh look at classroom situations and rethink how to deal with challenging situations. The RPG has helped me look at classroom challenges in a more objective way."

RPGs work well to increase teacher efficacy for two main reasons. The first is their collaborative, democratic nature. All participants have equal stature in the group. Experienced teachers share critical incidents in the same way that novice teachers do. Secondary teachers express concerns about classroom management similar to elementary teachers. The need for common goals becomes exceedingly clear when special education teachers talk with classroom teachers about student learning plans. The more teachers across disciplines and grade levels talk with each other, the greater understanding they have of the big picture.

The second reason why RPGs increase teacher efficacy is the open environment of the groups. RPGs are evaluation-free settings. This means that participants share their experiences without worrying that their jobs will be jeopardized as a result.

What does strong efficacy mean to the teachers in your school? There is reason to believe that this process leads to a constructivist form of teacher leadership. Linda Lambert provides an excellent description of constructivist leadership: "the reciprocal processes that enable participants in an educational community to construct meanings that lead toward a common purpose about schooling."[2]

Teacher leaders engage in leadership behavior even when their role does not identify them as "the leader." Lambert distinguishes between role leadership and acts of leadership. An act of leadership is the

> performance of actions (behavior plus intention) that enable participants in a community to evoke potential within a trusting environment, to reconstruct or break set with old assumptions, to focus on the construction of meaning, or to frame actions based on new behaviors and purposeful intention. Everyone in the school community can perform an act of leadership.[3]

This formula for a trusting environment in which colleagues work together to construct meaning and challenge old assumptions is put into action in RPGs. When teachers have the opportunity to engage in this type of professional activity, they comment:

> "I have become more empathetic to other teachers—more able to look outside myself and therefore have become a better team member."

"I find myself teaming more and asking for the perspectives of others and ultimately this pays off in improved student performance and to the collaborative effort."

Jennifer York-Barr, William Sommers, Gail Ghere, and Jo Montie agree that reflective practice leads to higher teacher efficacy, which in turn leads to increased student learning.

In education, the desired outcomes are increases in student learning and capacity to learn, with learning broadly conceptualized as including academic, social, and emotional well-being. High levels of student learning require high levels of staff competence. Reflective practice increases the potential of schools to improve for at least the following reasons:

- It increases the *opportunity to continuously learn* from and about educational practice. If educators do not reflect on and learn from their practice, they are likely to continue doing what they have been doing.
- Practitioners have a *greater variety of perspectives* to draw on in addressing the many challenging and complex dilemmas of practice. Consideration of perspectives can result in more effective solutions, which are more broadly understood, accepted, and implemented.
- *New knowledge and understandings* that have immediate applications to practice are created. Knowledge constructed within the context of practice is needed to effectively teach the increasing variety of school-age children and youth. By sharing newly constructed knowledge among colleagues, the impact for improvement can be multiplied.
- *Efficacy* increases as educators see the positive effects on their own context-generated solutions. Efficacy refers to the belief that one can make a difference in the lives of students. As the internal capacities of teachers are recognized and tapped, a greater sense of empowerment emerges.
- Professional educators themselves assume *personal responsibility for learning* and improvement. Rather than relying on the system for training programs to substantially improve or fix the instructional process, educators come to rely on themselves and one another.
- *Strengthened relationships and connections* among staff members emerge. As continuous improvement becomes a shared goal and reflection becomes embedded in practice, isolation is reduced, and relationships strengthen, giving rise to a foundation for schoolwide improvement.
- Educators can build *bridges between theory and practice.* They consider externally generated knowledge from the research community and then

determine appropriate, customized applications or combinations of appli-cations to their specific context of practice.

- *A reduction in external mandates* may ultimately result when educators are viewed as effectively addressing many of the challenges of practice. The belief that externally prescribed interventions must be mandated if schools are to improve could be challenged.[4]

M. Evans describes conditions under which adults learn best.[5] This makes an excellent bridge to reflective practice. Adults use a construc-tivist approach to learning. They examine the new learning based on their previous experiences and schemata, which is framed against their previous knowledge of the topic. Together, this acts as a filter for new learning. Through ongoing problem solving and questioning in RPGs adults test their knowledge using processes of applications, abstraction, and generalization. Similarly, Dewey described this process as "a con-secutive ordering in such a way that each determines the next as its proper outcome, while each in turn leans back on its predecessors." [6] Adult learners move back and forth between new knowledge and pre-viously held knowledge. RPGs provide an arena for colleagues to reg-ularly and systematically construct new knowledge and challenge pre-viously held beliefs about our profession.

NOTES

1. Chase, Betsy, Richard Germundsen, Joan Cady Brownstein, and Linda Schaak Distad, "Making the Connection between Increased Student Learning and Reflective Practice," *Educational Horizons* 79 (2001): 3.

2. Linda Lambert. "Toward a Theory of Constructivist Leadership." In Linda Lambert, Deborah Walker, Diane P. Zinnerman, Joanne E. Cooper, Morgan Dale Lambert, Mary E. Gardner, and P. J. Ford Slack (eds.), *The Constructivist Leader* (New York: Teachers College Press, 1995), 29.

3. Linda Lambert, *Building Leadership Capacity in Schools* (Alexandria, Va.: Association for Supervision and Curriculum Development, 1998), 29.

4. Jennifer York-Barr, William A. Sommers, Gail S. Ghere, and Jo Montie. *Reflective Practice to Improve Schools* (Thousand Oaks, Calif.: Corwin, 2001), 8–9.

5. M. Evans, "Why Adults Learn in Different Ways," *Lifelong Learning: An Omnibus of Practice and Research* 57 (1987): 22–25, 27.

6. John Dewey, *How We Think* (Mineola, N.Y.: Dover Publications, 1920/1997), 2.

CHAPTER 4

Our Reflective Practice Groups

In our initial project with Reflective Practice Groups (RPGs), we tried to create a cross-section of the district within each group. Each group consisted of ten to twelve educators including beginning teachers, teachers new to the district, mentors, experienced teachers, and administrators. When possible, each group had teachers from the elementary, middle, and secondary levels. We also encouraged the specialists to join. Most groups included a physical education teacher, an English Language Learner teacher (English as a second language teacher), a music teacher, an art teacher, or a special education teacher. Their presence broadened the discussions.

Each RPG was assigned a primary group facilitator. We used education department faculty members from area colleges as group facilitators. This worked well because their involvement closed the loop of teacher development—from preservice to in-service. However, district personnel such as those involved with faculty development also worked well as group facilitators. The main responsibilities of the primary group facilitator were to convene the group, determine meeting dates and locations, and discuss group norms. Eventually, the facilitation of the group rotated among the group members, but the primary group facilitator assumed responsibility for the group's progress.

Groups met monthly from September to May for about two hours. Most groups met after school in one of the school buildings; however, a few groups chose to meet off-site. Those that did found an off-site location very relaxing but sometimes difficult to arrange. Another challenge associated with going outside the school building is the need for confidentiality. The group needs to meet in an area allowing for privacy and professionalism. (We had a rule that no alcohol could be served in the location.) Groups that met off campus arranged for a setting that had free, private, meeting rooms that could be reserved. The groups that met at school chose classrooms or faculty lounges. In some instances, groups decided to rotate locations so that members could experience various buildings and classroom environments.

Over the years, we have worked with several districts and in each case their expectations differed somewhat. One district offered a small stipend to those who volunteered to participate in RPGs. Another district stated that involvement by new teachers and their mentors was required. Districts that did not offer compensation arranged to have teachers meet during previously scheduled faculty development times. Teachers in our project earned graduate credit for their participation in reflective practice.

In order to have a strong beginning, all RPGs in the district met together as a group for an orientation session in early September. We set aside about two hours for the orientation. After a brief introduction to the history of reflective practice and the district's expectations, the teachers moved into their small groups. These groups were formed by the induction-year committee of the district.

OVERVIEW OF THE REFLECTIVE PRACTICE GROUP PROCESS

A preliminary step in the process was to convene the group and establish rules for how the group would function. We provided each participant with a copy of the RPG Process, a worksheet for writing down responses, and a group membership list with home and work phone numbers and e-mail addresses. Once these organizational matters were completed the group proceeded with the reflective practice process.

THE REFLECTIVE PRACTICE GROUP PROCESS

When the group is convened, the process proceeds as follows.

- Establish rules for how the group will function.
- Discuss confidentiality.
- Engage in the process detailed below.

1. Each person writes down a critical incident that she or he has experienced since the last meeting. Give the incident one of the following labels: Planning and Preparation, Classroom Environment, Instruction, or Professional Responsibilities.
2. Each person briefly shares his or her incident with the group. No embellishments or questions at this point.
3. The group chooses one of the shared incidents to discuss more fully.
4. The group asks the teller of the incident for more details — clarifying information, impact on others, teacher's feelings about the incident, and so on.
5. Each person writes down answers to the following questions: What are the beliefs about teaching and learning that help us to better understand this incident? Why was this an effective or ineffective approach?
6. Each person shares his or her responses to Step Five.
7. The group engages in a discussion of the following: What can you learn from this incident that will help you in future situations? Is the action you would take consistent with the image that you want to project of who you are as a teacher?
8. The group facilitator summarizes the discussion.

Step One: *Each person writes down a critical incident that she or he has observed or experienced recently. Give the incident one of the following labels: Planning and Preparation, Classroom Environment, Instruction, or Professional Responsibilities.*

The incident could have either a positive or negative focus. The important factor was that the incident caused the participant to question some aspect of his or her practice. We used a simple worksheet to keep the RPG process on task. Participants wrote their critical incidents in the top box of the worksheet and circled the appropriate label(s). We allowed five to ten minutes for everyone to write down one incident and used Charlotte Danielson's four domains as categories to organize the critical incidents.[1] We also considered INTASC Standards,[2] National Board for Professional Teaching Standards' Core Propositions,[3] or state standards for teachers as potential organizing frameworks.

Reflective Practice Group Worksheet

Critical Incident:

Choose a label for your incident: Planning and Preparation

Classroom Environments

Instruction

Professional Responsibilities

What can you learn from this incident that will help you in future situations? Is the action you would take consistent with the image that you want to project as a teacher?

Notes:

Step Two: Each person briefly shares their incident with the group. No embellishments or questions are allowed at this point.

Each participant succinctly explained his or her incident in less than two minutes. The purpose of this step was to give an overview of what was happening in the lives of the participants.

Step Three: The group chooses one of the shared incidents to discuss more fully.

Because time did not allow the group to discuss thoroughly all the shared incidents, it was necessary to choose one incident. Urgency or the emergence of a theme helped to determine the choice of incident. The selected incident or theme became the incident of the group rather than that of the individual teacher. Shared ownership of the incident allowed everyone to discuss the incident more freely.

Step Four: The group asks the teller of the incident for more details— clarifying information, impact on others, and the teacher's feelings about the incident.

After everyone in the RPG had an opportunity to ask clarifying questions and the teacher had thoroughly conveyed the details of the incident, the group moved to Step Five.

Step Five: Each person writes down answers to the following questions: What are the beliefs about teaching and learning that help us to better understand this incident? Why was this an effective or ineffective approach?

In box three of the Reflective Practice Group Worksheet, participants were asked to consider and write down the theories and beliefs about teaching and learning that were relevant to the chosen incident or theme. Participants were also asked to consider the effectiveness or ineffectiveness of the handling of the classroom incident.

Whether experienced teachers or first-year novices, most teachers in our groups had difficulty identifying the educational theories that drive their actions. Yet as teachers we challenge ourselves to ask the important questions. Why is it that we value the relationship between parent and teacher? Why do we spend so much time attending to our students' psychological and emotional needs rather than just attending to their cognitive development? How can we teach each student in our classes so that his or her learning needs are best met? These questions are not easy. Although teachers are clearly scholars in their fields, they tend to avoid a formal examination of the research base that informs their practice. The educational values and tenets to which most teachers subscribe do not surface in most discussions between colleagues. The research base for educational practice goes unnamed and unchallenged. It is the purpose of Step Five to examine these values and tenets.

Step Six: Each person shares his or her responses to Step Five.

Throughout the RPG process, individual responses by all group members are valued. After about ten minutes of writing, everyone shared their ideas about the educational theories that were at the heart of the incident. We moved clockwise around the table.

Often during this portion of the process, participants were unsure about what was meant by "beliefs about teaching," but when common beliefs or theories were explained, it gave teachers confidence to move forward with the discussion. What resulted was a highly charged professional discussion linking theory to practice.

By attaching an educational theory to our beliefs we honor the work that has come before us and attach importance to our work as scholars in our profession. As professionals, it is our responsibility to continually examine and challenge the research base and revise it when appropriate. The popularity of Action Research in schools has helped to move this process along.

John Smyth explains the importance of teachers theorizing.

Where teaching is conceived as a static process of transmitting accepted bodies of knowledge, and where the "ends" of teaching are artificially divorced from the "means," there are continual problems about how to translate somebody else's theory into practice. By using concrete and practical experience with all its frustrations and contradictions as the basis upon which to theorize, teachers become agents in the creation of their own structures of knowledge in regard to a range of matters, including subject matter and curricular content, classroom organization, strengths and weaknesses in their teaching, along with the interests and needs of students.[4]

The next step was the one that most participants wanted to discuss first—what are some solutions to this problem? Then, what can be learned from this incident? But most importantly, is the action that you would take consistent with the image that you want to project of yourself as a teacher?

Step Seven: The group engages in a discussion of the following: What can you learn from this incident that will help you in future situations? Is the action you would take consistent with the image that you want to project of who you are as a teacher?

Most groups wanted to begin the RPG process by jumping right to providing solutions to the problem. This tendency is probably due to the fact that teachers problem solve all day long. According to some research, teachers make, on the average, a thousand decisions each day.[5] All of these quick decisions are necessary to maintain a smooth-running, safe, productive classroom environment. But RPGs are designed to emphasize reflection!

Step Eight: The group facilitator summarizes the discussion.

At the conclusion of each meeting, the group facilitator took a few minutes to summarize the day's discussion, which helped the group to focus on the lessons learned that day.

In the next chapter, we further examine the benefits of RPGs.

NOTES

1. Charlotte Danielson, *Enhancing Professional Practice: A Framework for Teachers* (Alexandria, Va.: Association for Supervision and Curriculum Development, 1996).

2. Model Standards for Beginning Teacher Licensing and Development: A Resource for State Dialogue (www.ccso.org/intasc.html).

3. National Board for Professional Teaching Standards (www.nbpts.org).

4. John Smyth, *Critical Perspectives on Educational Leadership* (London: Falmer Press, 1989), 188.

5. Philip W. Jackson, *Life in Classrooms* (New York: Teachers College Press: Columbia University, 1990).

CHAPTER 5

What We Learned from Reflective Practice Groups

After each Reflective Practice Group (RPG) meeting, the college participants wrote up a summary of their group's activities using a standard reporting format. As a result, we documented 1,073 critical incidents and 144 case studies. The incidents are the brief descriptions of an event that everyone in the group shared in Step Two. The case studies are the full development of the Reflective Group Process around the selected incidents from each session. The data from three years of reflective groups were organized by month and year using the following codes.

- curriculum and teaching
- student academic issues
- student behavior
- student-teacher issues
- student-teacher-family issues
- student-to-student conflicts
- systemic policy issues
- teacher role/responsibility concerns
- parent-teacher issues
- teacher-colleague issues

The coded data are stored in an electronic data base available at http://minerva.stkate.edu/academic/educcases.nsf.

Through our work with RPGs, we learned that: (1) teachers experience predictable phases of development over the school year; (2) behavior management and relationships with parents and colleagues are

Survival	Disillusionment	Rejuvenation	Reflection
September	October November December	January February March	April May

Figure 5.1.   *Predictable Stages in the Lives of Teachers*

dominant issues for teachers; and (3) the link between theory and practice is often a difficult coupling for teachers.

PREDICTABLE STAGES IN THE LIVES OF TEACHERS

Moir and Stubbe report that new teachers go through the predictable phases of anticipation before the school year begins, and survival, disillusionment, rejuvenation, and reflection phases during the academic year.[1] In our experience with RPGs, we found that new and experienced teachers went through similar phases, but the experienced teachers went through them more quickly, as shown in Figure 5.1.

SURVIVAL PHASE

September or October was the first month of RPGs, depending on the school calendar. During this time, everyone was expending a lot of energy in an effort to establish a reasonable classroom/school climate and to define boundaries. In fact, most new teachers felt overwhelmed and were functioning at a reactive level with little time for reflection. In our initial project, the topic of "student behavior" was the largest percentage of incidents presented by Reflective Practice Group participants. However, the percentage of critical incidents selected for group discussion was equally divided between "student-teacher-family," "parent-teacher," and "student behavior" in October. Our experience was consistent with the "Survival" phase.

DISILLUSIONMENT PHASE

During the months of October, November, and December, the extensive time commitment and the rigor of the job led to low teacher morale. Although "student behavior" continued to be the dominant issue of teachers and RPGs, concerns spanned a much broader range of issues including "student-academic" issues as well as territorial conflicts between teachers and challenges to the district's policies and procedures.

REJUVENATION PHASE

After winter break, teachers returned from the holidays with a sense of energy and excitement about the final months of the school year. Yet the rejuvenation stage is also fraught with recurring stresses including "student behavior." Teachers and groups dealt with an increasing array of "systemic-policy," "teacher role and responsibility," "teacher-colleague," "parent-teacher," "student-academic," and "curriculum and teaching" issues.

REFLECTION PHASE

In April and May, the teachers looked back at the school year and their teaching. They analyzed the highs and lows of the school year and anticipated the next year. In contrast, some first-year teachers received letters stating that their contracts would not be renewed. Groups focused on "student-academic," "student-behavior," "student-teacher-family," "teacher-colleague," "systemic-policy," "teacher role and responsibility," and "curriculum and teaching" concerns.

The rhythms of the school year are important to keep in mind when working with new teachers. What seemed so difficult in the beginning of the year seemed easier at the end of the year. When teachers are in the survival mode, it is difficult to step back and think of alternative ways to manage difficult classroom situations. We found that Reflective Practice Groups provided the support of others through the phases of teaching and accelerated the practice of reflection.

DOMINANCE OF STUDENT BEHAVIOR AND RELATIONSHIPS WITH PARENTS AND COLLEAGUES

In reviewing the critical incidents and case studies, we were struck by the emotional tone of teachers when they felt powerless, challenged, and ignored. The situations and case studies generally represented the second and fourth domains of Charlotte Danielson's *Framework for Teaching*.[2] The largest percentage of critical incidents presented by teachers during every month and year except for March and April were in Domain 2: Classroom Environment (53.5 percent). The March and April exceptions reflected Domain 4: Professional Responsibilities (38.4 percent). New teachers felt more prepared to plan and teach lessons but did not feel prepared to handle situations beyond their immediate control or with challenging students, parents, and colleagues.

However, the prevalence of incidents in Domains 2 and 4 provides learning opportunities for revealing the connections between planning and instruction (Domains 1 and 3). Teachers can examine whether or not they are using practices that reflect the best knowledge available on teaching and learning. They can also determine if their practices are consistent with their teaching beliefs.

THEORY-PRACTICE DILEMMA

According to Stansbury and Zimmerman, "in the short run, beginning teachers profit by solving particular problems; but in the long run, they profit by knowing how to think constructively about any problem that comes up in their teaching."[3] Hiebert, Gallimore, and Stigler frame the theory-practice chasm as the divide between professional knowledge and practitioner knowledge. Professional knowledge is "public, storable, and sharable, and serves as a mechanism for verification and improvement in teaching." Practitioner's knowledge is linked to practice— "detailed, concrete, specific and integrated."[4]

Typically, groups found the most difficult step in the process to be discussing professional knowledge and theory. The tendency of teachers was to offer suggestions for solving another teacher's problem. The following debriefing comment illustrates this situation:

> We kept close to the process. Group members wanted to comfort the teacher immediately. We found it difficult to draw on relevant theory.

However, there were also examples of groups who had quite remarkable discussions during the theory step, as the following quote shows.

The most common way for children to learn socialization skills and appropriate behavior is through observation of others (Social Learning Theory). However, in this instance, there seems to be some indication that the home may not have provided early models of appropriate behavior and as a result, the social development delay. The child also seems to have strong attention needs that are not met in positive ways, so he has learned that he does get attention when he behaves inappropriately and thus this behavior is what is reinforced. When these patterns are learned, they are hard to change, requiring shaping and other cognitive behavioral methods to establish new patterns so that the child begins to be rewarded for appropriate behaviors and these behaviors replace the negative ones.

Britzman among others addresses the "dramatic shift" for beginning teachers as they move from the university setting to teaching in real classrooms. Traditionally, a disconnect between theory and practice formed because beginning teachers were not given adequate support for thinking about their practice and how theory is an interpretation of their experience. Beginning teachers must transform their university knowledge about teaching as well as their identity from student to teacher. Theory and reflection aid the constant refinement of their professional knowledge.[5]

The difficulty of our participants to articulate their research-based beliefs about teaching and learning led to changes in our reflection process. We added facilitator's comments and updates on the previous case studies. College facilitators also brought in articles or ideas for further exploration of applicable theory regarding the previous reflective practice group. These additions to our reflective process further developed professional knowledge and additional solutions to critical classroom incidents. We believe that teachers who have the predisposition to develop a deep knowledge of teaching and learning will not be satisfied with recipes or bags of tricks.

NOTES

1. E. Moir and C. Stubbe, "Professional Growth for New Teachers: Support and Assessment through Collegial Partnership," *Teacher Education Quarterly* 22 (fall 1995).

2. Charlotte Danielson, *Enhancing Professional Practice*.

3. Kendyll Stansbury and Joy Zimmerman, *Lifelines to the Classroom: Designing Support for Beginning Teachers* (San Francisco: West End, 2000), 5.

4. James Hiebert, Robert Gallimore, and James W. Stigler, "A Knowledge Base for the Teaching Profession: What It Looks Like, and How Can We Get One?" *Educational Researcher* 31(2002): 6, 7–8.

5. Deborah P. Britzman, *Practice Makes Practice: A Critical Study of Learning to Teach* (Albany: State University of New York Press, 1991).

CHAPTER 6

An Exemplary Reflective Practice Session

At a Reflective Practice Group (RPG) meeting in September, the following incidents were shared:

STEPS ONE AND TWO: CRITICAL INCIDENTS

- A middle-school girl who is very popular is also very talkative and disruptive in class. She is very respectful and polite when the teacher intervenes but she persists in interrupting the class. (Classroom Environment)
- A middle-school boy is disruptive in class. He talks with his friend regardless of the friend's physical proximity to him. This is a constant problem for the class. (Classroom Environment)
- A middle-school girl has not yet turned in any of her assignments for this school year. Her mother wrote a letter to the teacher requesting that her daughter be excused from all of the missed work. (Professional Responsibilities)
- An eighth-grade class will be phased out due to school reorganization. A new teacher is assigned to the class for this year. The teacher is having difficulty being accepted by the students. (Classroom Environment)
- A girl in language arts class is continually seeking attention during class. On one particular day, she insisted that she had a problem with her eye and yet the school nurse could not find anything wrong. Her distress about her eye led to a fit of crying during which she also complained that her mother is never available to

her. The girl's father died the year before. (Classroom Environment)

- A boy consistently does not turn in his work. The teacher called the boy's parents and tried to work out a plan for completing the outstanding work. The boy is in danger of failing the class. (Instruction)
- A blue-haired boy is loitering in the common area of the school after the bell has rung to commence the day. As a teacher escorts him to his homeroom, they exchange angry and unproductive remarks. (Professional Responsibilities)
- An LD teacher is trying classroom adaptations with one of her students. The student, however, is very passive—he shows no emotion; often he has a blank stare; no assignments are completed either from inside or outside class. (Planning and Preparation)
- A middle-level student, while working on a chemistry assignment, used a Bunsen burner in a dangerous manner. The new teacher disciplined the student and then called the student's mother. When she didn't reach the mother at home, she called her at work and left a message with the mother's coworker. The mother was upset about being called at work and she was enraged that the new teacher left the message with a coworker. (Classroom Environment; Professional Responsibilities)
- A special-education child, who is new to the district, is not participating in any way. No services are in place for him because his paperwork has not yet arrived in the district. The child's goal in life is to become a "couch potato." (Instruction)

STEPS THREE AND FOUR: THE DETAILED ACCOUNT OF THE CHOSEN INCIDENT

The group selected the incident of the middle-level science teacher and asked the teacher for more details. The new teacher shared that a middle-level student, while working on a chemistry assignment, used a Bunsen burner in a dangerous manner. The new teacher disciplined the student and then called the student's mother. When she didn't reach the mother at home, she called her at work and left a message with the mother's coworker. The mother was upset about being called at work and she was enraged that the new teacher left the message with a coworker. The new teacher and the mother had a heated exchange of words with both using less than professional language. The entire focus of the phone call was forgotten. What started out as the teacher reacting responsibly and appropriately to a dangerous behavior ended with her fearing that she might lose her job. The teacher was worried because the parent was going to contact the principal about her use of inappropriate language and the breach of confidentiality by leaving a public message at the parent's work setting.

This new teacher needed guidance immediately. Fortunately, the RPG process gave her a vehicle for sharing the incident without fear of reprisal. Group members assisted her as she developed a plan for refocusing concern on the dangerous behavior and salvaging her relationships with the student, the parent, and her principal.

STEPS FIVE AND SIX: DISCUSSION OF TEACHING BELIEFS AND THE APPROACH

The teacher had numerous concerns. First, she wanted to maintain a safe learning environment for all of her students. Second, she was concerned about setting an example for the students both directly and indirectly involved with the incident. She wanted everyone to understand the seriousness and the potentially long-lasting implications of inappropriate behavior in a chemistry laboratory. Third, she wanted to ensure that this behavior was not repeated.

By involving the student's parent, she was following a preestablished disciplinary plan for infractions in the lab. Up to this point, she was pleased with how she had handled the incident. She had called the mother at home but there was no answer. Believing that the seriousness of the incident required immediate contact with the mother, she called the mother's work setting. The mother was on her break, so the teacher told the person who answered that "Brad had had a problem at school and Mrs. Smith should call his chemistry teacher as soon as possible." The coworker took some delight in this and conveyed the message by broadcasting it over the office announcement system. The mother was humiliated and enraged. She felt that all information about her son was confidential and should not be shared with anyone other than herself. When the mother returned the call she was so upset about the manner in which the message had been conveyed that she never listened to the content. The mother accused the teacher of being unprofessional and incompetent. The conversation escalated until the mother was screaming and swearing into the phone. After several minutes of trying to refocus the conversation, the teacher lost her composure and said, "What the heck can I do about it now?" This attitude gave the mother even more reason to believe that the teacher was incompetent and unprofessional. As soon as the words left the teacher's mouth she regretted them. She apologized but the mother was too incensed to hear her. The mother's next step was to call the principal. The principal listened carefully to the mother's concerns but did not react to her. Fortunately, the principal was experienced at dealing with explosive situations. He told the mother that he would sit down with her after he had spoken with the teacher. The meeting with the principal and the teacher had not yet taken place.

The fallout from this incident touched numerous areas. The entire focus of concern shifted from dangerous behavior by a student in a chemistry lab to unprofessional behavior by a new teacher. The teacher was faced with having to explain her behavior to her principal. Because it was only September, this was the first real encounter the new teacher was going to have with the principal. She was worried that she might lose her job. The teacher felt that she had not yet established her credibility and effectiveness as a teacher. The principal would only have this experience to draw from. Needless to say, it was a painful situation for the new teacher to deal with so early in her career. And to make matters even worse, the real cause for the encounter had not been addressed!

Three educational theories surfaced. Many of the group participants believed that communication between parents and teachers is an essential component of the student success formula. They cited the work of Joyce Epstein in addition to giving examples from their own experiences to support their beliefs. Several participants stated that it is the teacher's responsibility to maintain a safe learning environment for all students. They referred to the state's code of ethics for teachers. The third response from the group was the area of teacher professionalism.

Once again, the state's code of ethics was cited and also Danielson's Fourth Domain.

STEP SEVEN: ALTERNATIVE STRATEGIES

The group participants were able to offer some constructive advice to the new teacher. Fortunately, several participants knew the principal well and believed that he was a reasonable professional. This knowledge was comforting to the new teacher who was afraid that she might lose her job over the incident. The solutions that the group offered were:

1. Document all aspects of the incident. Begin with the incident in the chemistry laboratory and include the teacher's conduct on the telephone with the parent.
2. Sit down with the student and create a re-entry plan. It is important to bring the focus back to ensuring safety in the chemistry laboratory.
3. Call the parent with a follow-up plan for the student's return to the chemistry laboratory. Call the parent at home, ensuring that her privacy is respected. Begin by apologizing for allowing the conversation to take such a negative turn but then redirect the focus of the conversation to the behavior in the chemistry lab. Explain that teacher and student have created a plan for his behavior in the lab and that the situation is resolved and everyone can now move forward.

The RPG participants emphasized that it is important that the teacher close the communication loop with the parent and re-establish herself as a professional.

STEP EIGHT: FACILITATOR COMMENTS

The RPG process helped the new teacher deconstruct a very painful and embarrassing experience. However, with the help of her colleagues, she learned how to avoid similar conflicts. She also stepped back and examined who she wanted to be as a teacher. When she called the mother to discuss the student's behavior, she did so because she believed that communication between the parent and teacher is essential. She also believed that it was her professional responsibility to apprise the mother of the student's behavior. However, the manner in which she responded to the mother was not consistent with the image she wanted to project as a teacher. This was very disappointing to the teacher.

In the future, the teacher will work on maintaining a positive, constructive demeanor in her exchanges with people—students, colleagues, and parents. Because she tends to "fly off the handle" when under duress, she is going to calm herself before potentially volatile encounters. If she sees that they are moving in a negative direction, she will end the discussion and make an appointment for a later date. The support of her RPG helped this new teacher to return to the classroom the next day.

CHAPTER 7

How to Set Up Your Own Reflective Practice Groups

First, it is important to determine who will participate in the Reflective Practice Groups (RPGs). Will you only include first-year teachers? Will all the teachers be from one building? Will you group teachers by discipline or grade level? In our experience, the most successful groups create a microcosm of the district.

A group of ten to twelve participants is ideal because it generates a lively and diverse discussion. The group should include several beginning teachers and their mentors, several experienced teachers, and a group facilitator. When forming our groups we used a broad definition to identify "new" teachers. We included those who were new to the district, those who had changed grade levels or subject areas, and those who were re-entering the profession after a time away.

In all cases, it is critical that the district's expectations are clearly stated and understood at the beginning. Groups function best if the participants are enthusiastic about the process. If participants feel that they are being coerced into attending they often bring negative, nonproductive attitudes to the experience. It is better to start with willing participants and let their excitement about the process have a contagious affect on others in the building.

One of the main goals for the first session is to establish rapport with group participants. After the large group has heard the brief history of the reflective practice process and the district expectations have been explained, it is time to break into RPGs. The groups should be organized prior to the meeting. Remember, it is during this process that you will need to decide how your groups will be configured. Each group will need to be assigned a room in which to meet. Classrooms work very well; they are roomy, private, and convenient. You will also need to identify a primary group facilitator.

The primary group facilitator will lead the group on the first day and for the next one to two sessions. This person will also be the point person in case issues arise between sessions. For example, if it becomes necessary to unexpectedly cancel a session, the primary group facilitator would initiate a process for communicating with the group's participants. After the group has met a few times, the facilitation of the group should rotate among members. The primary group facilitator then becomes a mentor to the session facilitators.

Once the group is gathered in its meeting space, it is time to get to know each other. The primary group facilitator should model the introduction process. With participants arranged in a circle, ask everyone to say a few words about themselves. Participants want to hear about each other's professional lives (how many years they have taught, the grade levels, subject areas, etc.) but they also want to get to know each other as whole persons. Each participant should talk about an aspect of their personal lives that they are comfortable sharing. Many people will talk about their children or their hobbies. Anything is fine. The purpose is to begin to establish rapport and build trust between group members. This will be important when participants share critical events in their teaching.

In order for the RPG process to work effectively, participants must feel comfortable and welcome in the group. Part of that involves ensuring that everyone is treated in a positive and respectful manner.

After each participant has introduced him or herself, the group should decide what norms to follow in order that the atmosphere remains positive, supportive, and productive. For example, most groups agree that arriving on time for each session is very important. So punctuality might be a group norm. Notifying another group member when they are unable to attend might also be a group norm. Depending on the personality or the needs of the group, the primary group facilitator may also identify norms that are essential for the effective functioning of the group. In addition to the group's list, there are some nonnegotiable norms.

Confidentiality is crucial for the effective functioning of all groups. Participants must feel confident that they can speak freely within their group. RPG participants must not discuss events outside the confines of the RPG meetings. They must also feel that they can speak without fear of judgment by other group members. Like all professional discussions, names of particular individuals should not be used whenever possible. We recognize, however, that it is impossible to do this all the time and that is why it is so important that total confidentiality be maintained within the group.

On the lighter side, we have found that providing food at the RPG meetings helps participants to relax. We distribute a "treat sheet" at the orientation meeting. Everyone in the group signs up to bring a small treat to share at each meeting. Both something to eat and a beverage work well. While some of these items may seem trivial, all of these decisions add to the positive performance of the Reflective Practice Groups.

Like all new processes, it is important to have a strong beginning. We accomplished this by having all the groups from the district meet together at an orientation session in early September. Try to set aside about two hours for the orientation. The purpose of this meeting is to:

1. Provide a brief history of reflective practice.
2. Explain district expectations for group participation.
3. Introduce group participants.
4. Establish group norms.
5. Provide an overview of the reflective practice process.

Do not be disappointed if you are not able to actually "do" reflective practice at the orientation session. Establishing a strong foundation is the goal and you will be grateful for all efforts devoted to making this happen. However, even if the time is short, at least provide the participants with an overview of the RPG process. Most participants are very curious about this new commitment. To allay their fears, it is important to walk through the process. Follow the eight-step process and use the accompanying worksheet to keep the group focused.

CHAPTER 8

Case Studies for Further Exploration

Now that you understand the concept and process of Reflective Practice Groups (RPGs), we would like to provide opportunities for you to try out your problem-solving strategies using sample case studies from our database of RPGs. The critical incidents in this chapter introduce classroom situations spanning the phases of teacher concerns over the school year as well as domains of instruction. You will have the opportunity to make theory to practice connections and suggest alternative solutions to these real classroom incidents. You will find the case studies helpful in exploring your personal beliefs about and knowledge of teaching and learning.

CASE STUDY 1: WANDERING STUDENT AND MIXED MESSAGES FROM THE PRINCIPAL

The middle-level teacher in the following incident is concerned because he feels that the school administrator is giving inconsistent messages to a student. The teacher has labeled the incident as "Professional Responsibility." This incident was discussed in October, which is the time of year when many teachers are experiencing feelings of disillusionment. They are finding that the role of teacher is much more complicated than they had anticipated and they are feeling stretched in multiple directions.

The Critical Incident

A student wanders into the teacher's classroom during class and doesn't belong there. When questioned by the teacher, the student says he has been talking with his dean and is on his way back to class. The student does not have a hall pass. The teacher asks him to leave. Ten minutes later, the teacher sees the student again and says, "I'll walk you back to class." At this point the student bolts from the classroom. The teacher follows and asks the student to stop but he continues. The teacher says, "Stop now and it won't be a big deal." The student continues walking a while longer with the teacher in pursuit. The teacher finally stops and returns to his classroom, where he asks his students who the truant student is. His students don't want to tell but eventually he finds out the student's name.

Later, he goes to the dean's office to report the student and finds him with the dean. The dean reports to the teacher that the truant student is in the habit of wandering around the building a lot. She says that he may not know that what he is doing is wrong. She asks the teacher to write up the situation.

The teacher resents the amount of work it takes to write up a student. He does not trust that this student will face any consequences for his behavior. The teacher feels consequences are important for this kind of behavior, not only for the truant student but also as an example for other students to reinforce that such behavior is not tolerated.

Why do you think the teacher was upset by this incident?

What are the beliefs about teaching and learning that help you to better understand this incident?

During the discussion of Case Study 1, the RPG participants shared the following beliefs about teaching and learning:

- Teachers should be respected.
- The environment in schools needs to be managed and controlled by the adults in charge.
- Adults should know what to do and be able to do it.
- Actions speak louder than words.
- When you treat someone respectfully, as the teacher did, the other person should respond in kind.

How did you react to the incident? How do your beliefs compare to the RPG participants'?

What are solutions that you would try given what you know about best practice and theory?

If you would like to learn more about the topic discussed in Case Study 1, you will find the following resources helpful. We have included Internet links for a sampling of resources available from the Educator's Reference Desk (http://www.eduref.org).

Teaching Today

"The mission of Teaching Today is to give secondary teachers practical strategies and materials that encourage and inspire excellence and innovation in teaching."

http://www.glencoe.com/sec/teachingtoday/

Schoolwide and Classroom Discipline

"From NWREL's School Improvement Research Series"

http://www.nwrel.org/scpd/sirs/5/cu9.html

The RPG offered the following solutions. The "Comments" section includes general reflections on that day's RPG meeting.

Solutions

- Rather than follow the student himself, the teacher could have asked another adult to do so.
- The teacher could have ignored the situation and either let the student stay or sent him on his way.

Comments

Discussion of alternatives revealed that communication among adults in this setting needs some improvement. It is not clear to teachers what kind of behavior is expected of them in the face of recalcitrant and disrespectful students. It is also not clear what happens once a student is reported to a dean. Not only are the consequences unclear, but also teachers do not receive follow-up information on the student. Other students, however, know what happened because of the student grapevine. Teachers are out of the information loop. It also was suggested that the school might want to purchase walkie-talkies for principals and deans to make them more accessible to the immediate needs of teachers and students, especially in emergency situations.

What did you learn from Case Study 1?

CASE STUDY 2: THE OFF-TASK SIXTH GRADER

During the disillusionment phase, a typical teacher uncovers individual learning problems including skill deficits, poor work habits, and lack of motivation. In the following incident, a sixth grade teacher presents her observations of a student who is totally uninvolved in his school work.

The Critical Incident

A sixth grade student is not turning in any of his work. He appears to be "just there." He is not assertive nor is he disruptive. He has none of the needed tools—no pencil, paper, etc. Last year the boy was on Ritalin but the family does not want the medication to resume. The boy's parents work alternating schedules making a family conference difficult to schedule. An arranged meeting with his father did not take place. The teacher is very concerned because she feels that the boy has the ability to meet with some success in school. She is unsure of how to motivate him.

What are the signs of disengagement and what might be the contributing factors?

What are the beliefs about teaching and learning that help you to better understand this incident?

During the discussion of Case Study 2, the RPG participants discussed the relevance of the following theories:

- The sense of belonging
- Maslow's Hierarchy of Needs
- Importance of parental support (Comer, Epstein)
- Whole child theories (effects of physiological factors)

- Positive reinforcement
- Development psychology
- Perspectives on the use of medication for behavior control

How do your teaching beliefs and knowledge compare to the RPG participants'?

What are solutions that you would try given what you know about best practice and theory?

If you would like to learn more about the topic discusses in Case Study 2, you will find the following resources helpful. We have included Internet links for a sampling of resources available from the Educator's Reference Desk (http://www.eduref.org).

Increasing Student Engagement and Motivation: From Time-on-Task to Homework (October 2000)
"This booklet offers practical strategies to help teachers promote student engagement in learning. Provided by the Northwest Regional Educational Laboratory."
http://www.nwrel.org/request/oct00/index.html

Hard Work and High Expectations: Motivating Students to Learn (June 1992)
"The conference on Hard Work and High Expectations brought together prominent researchers who addressed the topic of student motivation from different social, cultural, and instructional perspectives. Summaries of the critical elements of their findings and conclusions are incorporated in this booklet; summaries of selected papers are included at the end."
http://www.kidsource.com/kidsource/content3/work.expectations.k12
.4.html

Tools for Teaching: Motivating Students
"Identifies teaching strategies to promote learning and enhance student motivation."
http://teaching.berkeley.edu/bgd/motivate.html

Solutions for Handling 117 Misbehaviors
"An index of student behaviors including a description of the behavior, its effects, and common mistakes that may perpetuate the problem."
http://www.disciplinehelp.com/behindex/default.htm

The following solutions were offered by the RPG. The "Comments" section includes general reflections on that day's RPG meeting.

Solutions

- The expectations between home and school need to become more closely aligned.
- The student needs a more individualized approach.
- The teacher needs to be more nurturing with the boy.
- The teacher needs to be more direct about pointing out positive activities for the boy.
- The teacher needs to talk with the parents and create a more specific action plan.
- The teacher needs to try to relate to the child on a more personal level, and find out his interests, hobbies.
- Only one teacher should be contacting the parents.

Comments

Some of the group members seemed a little stumped about what incident they should share; some did not feel that they had a new incident. I encouraged them to share their previous incident as it had evolved since our last meeting.

When I asked which incident the group would like to discuss, the teller of the "Off Task Student" incident quickly asked that we discuss her story. She was very anxious to have the support of the RPG as she tried to problem-solve this situation. This time the group attempted to cite theories that were influencing their practice and decision making. I was a little skeptical about whether we would be able to do this effectively. In fact, this part of the process worked very smoothly. I think the group was encouraged about their own level of expertise in this area.

The research theories that the group cited as influencing their teaching decisions seem to also influence how they feel as teachers. The theory (Sagor, Werner, etc.) that describes the importance of a person's sense of belonging to a group that was offered as an explanation for the "Off Task" student's reluctance to comply with the class norms also may be influencing the teacher. Because it was a new teacher who told the story, it may be her own lack of confidence that she "belongs" to this group called teachers that is making her feel so unsure.

All of the literature tells teachers that a strong, collaborative relationship with parents is essential for school success. This teacher may be questioning the significance of this research for her situation. To her, the parents may represent more of an impediment to the solution of the problem than a source of help.

For the next meeting, one of the other group members (a mentor teacher) is going to facilitate the discussion. I was not sure that I would be able to entice anyone into taking this on but he seemed very anxious to try it out. I think this will add another interesting dimension to the experience, especially if the facilitation steadily moves among the group members.

At the conclusion of the meeting, one of the group members suggested that they follow-up on the previous meeting's events. So, beginning with the next meeting, we will start with an update by the teller of the previous month's incident. The group is very anxious to hear whether the process is actually producing some positive results in the classroom (I am, too)!

What did you learn from this case study?

CASE STUDY 3: THE OVERWHELMED FIRST-YEAR TEACHER

During the disillusionment phase, it is not uncommon for teachers and particularly, first year teachers, to feel out of control with their responsibilities. In Case Study 3, a new teacher describes her amazement at the extent of the professional responsibilities of a teacher.

The Critical Incident

The new teacher feels overwhelmed with all there is to do and all the expectations others have of her. Her concerns include: turning in weekly lesson plans, being observed, the meetings she has to attend, the expectations of parents, meeting individual students' needs, compacting the curriculum, and on top of everything, thinking she has to know it all as the expert.

She wonders what is most important, what can she let slide. There's the new curriculum, knowing procedures in the school (and the assumption that she does know the procedures) and time limitations to find out what she needs to know before the deadlines (unknown) pass her by.

Often she does not even know who or what to ask! Sometimes the expectations are not clear. She feels as though she is coming up short, she becomes anxious, then feels the pressure of not enough time, becomes frustrated and takes it out on the kids, the last people she wants to take it out on. Sometimes she gets so busy with so many things that she feels that she has nothing to give.

Some kids really wear her out as well, five of them really need one-on-one attention to succeed. Then there are the skills you did not learn about in school . . . how to negotiate with parents, the principal, other teachers, the kids; and how to make mistakes and fix them. Where does a personal life fit in with all this!

Can you relate to this teacher? Why or why not?

What are the beliefs about teaching and learning that help you to better understand this incident?

During the discussion of Case Study 3, the RPG participants discussed their underlying beliefs about the experience of this first-year teacher.

- Teaching is one of the few professions in which beginning teachers are expected to function as experts, to know all they need to know to meet the multiple needs and demands of the job.
- The apprenticeship (student teaching) is extraordinarily short, yet new teachers are expected to act as experts on the first day of the job.
- They have the same responsibilities and challenges of those with many years of experience.
- Teachers need to recognize that no matter how hard they try there is no way that they can or will be perfect. So to demand perfection of themselves is to ask for frustration and failure.
- It is okay not to be perfect and to let others know you aren't.
- Make lists. Prioritize.

Do you agree with these teachers' perspectives? Why? or Why not?

What are solutions that you would try given what you know about best practice and theory?

We have selected a couple of resources that may be helpful in learning more about the topic of the first year of teaching. We have included Internet links for a sampling of resources available from the Educator's Reference Desk (http://www.eduref.org).

Supporting Beginning Teachers: How Administrators, Teachers, and Policymakers Can Help New Teachers Succeed (May 2001)
"This booklet provides a synthesis of recent research, describes programs to support beginning teachers, and offers tips for helping new teachers thrive." Provided by the Northwest Regional Educational Laboratory.
http://www.nwrel.org/request/may01/index.html

Survival Guide for New Teachers
"Presents advice from award-winning first-year teachers on how to work with veteran teachers, parents, principals, and teacher educators."
http://www.ed.gov/teachers/become/about/survivalguide/index.html

The RPG participants suggested alternative ways do deal with the feelings of being overwhelmed by teaching.

Solutions

- KISS (Keep it simple, stupid). Choose only one area to elaborate on at a time.
- Use teachers' manuals, that's why you have them.
- When a great idea occurs in the middle of a lesson, write it down on a sticky note and use it next time you teach.
- Lesson plans don't need to be all that detailed. Just list the pertinent information needed. You can keep separate notes or lists (on post-it™ notes) with the extra details and reminders you need.
- Create a list: *what I'm not going to do.*
- Ask yourself, "Can you live with it the way it is?" "Can you control it?" Then make a decision on what to do or not to do.

- Reward yourself when you have accomplished something big.
- Document late assignments.
- Keep a calendar.
- Help kids learn about failure and accountability.
- Use some of the language from Cooperative Discipline when dealing with parents.
- Be very specific and insist that they are as well.
- Learn shortcuts, don't be afraid to ask.
- Focus on learning—yours and theirs.

Comments

Everyone felt strongly about and could relate to this critical incident. New and experienced teachers can feel overwhelmed at times; they try to come to grips with the pressures they put on themselves as well as those others put on them. Everyone contributed enthusiastically to the solutions with ideas that worked for them and everyone felt as though they had picked up some valuable tips and felt better just expressing their frustrations.

What did you learn from this case study?

CASE STUDY 4: THE UNIQUE SEVENTH GRADER

Teachers also face the social and emotional needs of students. In Case Study 4, the coordinator for gifted and talented students describes a particularly challenging seventh grader.

The Critical Incident

The teacher is the gifted/talented coordinator for her district. She is concerned about a seventh-grade student that she has been working with. Both his parents and his teachers identified the student as being at risk due to his uniqueness. In addition to scoring a 99 percent on an ability achievement test, the boy is very unusual in other ways, too. He is very small in stature and carries all of his school belongings with him all day in his backpack, making him an odd looking sight. He does not want to go to school. He is incredibly disorganized, has poor social skills and makes inappropriate comments (i.e., "I am a serial killer"). As a result, he has few, if any, friends. The other students in his classes frequently tease him. One of his teachers said that she is afraid to call on him because of his inappropriate and unpredictable comments. The teacher is concerned about what her role as a specialist should be.

What might be the underlying causes of this seventh grader's behavior?
What are the beliefs about teaching and learning that help you to better understand this incident?
The RPG participants focused their discussion on the following themes:

* Belonging
* Self-fulfilling prophecy
* Peer tutoring
* Learning styles theories
* Peer mentoring

What are solutions that you would try given what you know about best practice and theory?
Are these solutions consistent with your beliefs about teaching and learning?
If you would like to learn more about the topic discussed in Case Study 4, you will find the following resources helpful. We have included Internet links for a sampling of resources available from the Educator's Reference Desk (http://www.eduref.org).

Hoagies Gifted Education Page
"Includes articles, research, books, organizations, conferences, on-line
    support groups, academic programs, products, and organizations
    that support gifted education locally, nationally, and globally."
http://www.hoagiesgifted.org/

David C. Baird's Gifted Children Web Site
"This site, created by a retired teacher of the gifted, includes infor-
    mation on the needs and characteristics of gifted children. Also in-
    cludes ideas for parents and teachers."
http://www3.sympatico.ca/daba/gifted/index.html

Solutions

Participants in the RPG proposed the following solutions.

- A more individualized curriculum is needed for this student.
- The boy needs to feel that he "belongs" in this setting.
- He may need to feel more control over his learning—how would he design his day?
- He may not need other people in the traditional way; maybe he doesn't need to fit in.
- Positive outlets for his extraordinary talents should be recommended—scouting, Odyssey of the Mind, peer mentoring, and so on.
- The fact that his parents recently divorced may have had a big impact on him—this should be explored.

Comments

The routine seems to have been established for the group. They know what it is and accept it. Today, for the first time, one of the mentors acted as the group facilitator. I think it added to the entire process. It certainly made it easier for me to take better notes.

At the end of the session I asked for a volunteer for a facilitator for next month, reluctantly, another mentor agreed to give it a try. Then after the session, one of the mentees came up to me and volunteered to facilitate the January meeting. I was thrilled!

I was pleased because the incident that was discussed today was not one of the mentees'. An experienced teacher's incident was analyzed. I think this was an important learning event for everyone—this showed that support and guidance are needed throughout one's career.

I am in awe of the group's thoughtful and respectful responses to all of the incidents. These have certainly added to the participants' repertoire of information. The side comments and tangents are helpful, too.

Today, one of the more experienced teachers reminded the group that we are approaching a very stressful time of year for both students and faculty. Depression, tension, anxiety—all of these are more apparent during the holidays.

I had not wanted to go to the meeting today because there was quite a heavy snowstorm. It took me about an hour and a quarter to get there and then two-and-a-half hours to get home. I spent a half an hour just on a freeway ramp. Despite all that, I was very glad that I had gone. The session went really well. The group is coming together more now.

There is only one mentee that is still quite reticent. (I strongly identify with her. I know that I would have responded much as she does. She is pleasant and engaged but very quiet.) I am going to try to coax the process in a way that will encourage her to be more outwardly engaged. I am starting to feel more a part of the group, too.

What did you learn from this case study?

CASE STUDY 5: THE BRIGHT YET DISORGANIZED FIFTH GRADER

A fifth-grade teacher shared the following incident about a gifted but disorganized student in her class. She labeled the incident as "Professional Responsibility" because her concerns focus on the relationship between the student's parent and teacher. The teacher shared the incident in November, which is when "disillusionment" is at its peak.

The Critical Incident

This is a very bright fifth grade child. He tends to be disorganized and gets very upset and tense when he doesn't have his work done on time. The parent claims it's the teacher's fault. The consequences for a late paper are loss of 5 points. One day this week, the parent and child came into the classroom at the beginning of the day, both in tears, because he had a math problem he couldn't understand and neither could the mother and so he couldn't do it.

Often the mother will walk to the lockers, take off her son's coat and hang it up and then come into the room with the child and unpack his backpack for him at the beginning of the school day. She always has excuses for him: not having work is the school's fault, bad policy, teachers have favorites.

Recently she came into the room and was shouting at the teacher in front of the child, accusing the teachers of being cruel, ruining her child, that they were unfair and needed to take parenting class. This was a very personal attack on the teacher. This parent is very aware of what goes on in the classroom as she is a volunteer in the room (at a time that her son is not in the class).

There is a history of this problem from previous years. She is always threatening to change schools. In the past the principal has listened to the parent with patience and not done much about the situation.

This time the entire team went to the principal and told her of the verbal attack. She seems to see the seriousness of the problem and has scheduled a meeting with the parent and the gifted specialist to let the parent know that the team wants to help the child.

Consider this:

The teacher labeled this incident as "Professional Responsibility." While this is certainly true, it is also true that a closer look at "Planning and Preparation" would be helpful. Why would planning and preparation be involved in this incident?

What are the beliefs about teaching and learning that help you to better understand this incident?

Comments

The members of the RPG became actively engaged in this particular case study.

There is research that indicates that having parents actively involved results in the parents' increased support and positive attitude about the process of schooling. In this instance the attack on the teachers and the school in front of the child is most destructive and can have a reverse effect on his school progress.

The behavior of the parent enables the student to not accept responsibility for his unfinished work, promotes learned helplessness, and results in a decline both in self-concept and motivation.

Even though at this point the relationship between the parent and teacher is antagonistic, it is important to open communications on a more positive note, perhaps with a negotiator. The principal realizes the seriousness of the personal attacks and has supported the teacher in not putting up with any more verbal abuse, and has scheduled a meeting with other professionals; this is the ideal way to begin dealing with this situation.

Canter's communication theory in dealing with difficult parents suggests that you try to win parents over to your side. This can be helped with a neutral party mediator such as the special education facilitator, the school social worker, or the gifted education coordinator.

In *Up from Underachievement,* the author suggests reframing the roles of teachers and parents as coaches and has forms for the parent and teacher to fill out with suggestions for helping the child and the roles each should play, working toward agreement and shared responsibility. This can include avoiding the placing of blame, reframing the issues as to what the child needs to experience success, acknowledging the need for parent support and coaching to help with the solution of the problem, as well as the coaching support of the teacher, and coming to agreement on the strategies each will use.

When there is this much hostility on the part of the parent, it causes one to wonder what else is at issue here. The reactions of the parent are so out of proportion to the situation that it calls into question the home situation and problems the parent might be facing as well as serious concerns for the psychological well being of the child. For this reason, having the social worker present and possibly suggesting psychological testing during the meeting may be an idea. There might even be cause for calling child protection if the parent is verbally abusive to the child or about the child, with the full understanding that child protection may do nothing as they may not deem it threatening enough.

Knowing how important parent/school communications are and how some parents do not understand or appreciate appropriate boundaries or times or methods of communication, a school should develop norms, guidelines, and expectations for parent/teacher communications and carefully spell them out in the school handbook, so that if these guidelines are not being respected, the policy can be pointed out and enforced.

Because of the inappropriateness of the parent's involvement when she brings the child to school and helps him off with his jacket, etc., perhaps the social worker can provide her with materials that help her understand appropriate social and emotional development (Erikson's Stages, especially Autonomy vs. Shame and Doubt, Initiative vs. Guilt, and Industry vs. Inferiority). Teachers and parents could benefit from a review of parenting styles and their implications for children and teachers.

Are these solutions consistent with your beliefs about teaching and learning?

If you would like to learn more about the topic discussed in Case Study 5, you may find the following resources helpful. We have included Internet links for a sampling of resources available from the Educator's Reference Desk (http://www.eduref.org).

Increasing Student Engagement and Motivation: From Time-on-Task to Homework (October 2000).
"This booklet offers practical strategies to help teachers promote student engagement in learning. Provided by the Northwest Regional Educational Laboratory."
http://www.nwrel.org/request/oct00/index.html

Hard Work and High Expectations: Motivating Students to Learn (June 1992).
"The conference on Hard Work and High expectations brought together prominent researchers who addressed the topic of student motivation from different social, cultural, and instructional perspectives. Summaries of the critical elements of their findings and conclusions are incorporated in this booklet; summaries of selected findings are included at the end."
http://kidsource.com/kidsource/content3/work.expectations.k12.4.html

A Compendium of Research-Based Information on the Education of Gifted and Talented Students (March 1997) by Karen S. Logan, Mary G. Riaaz, E. Jean Gubbins. M. Katherine Gavin, Valentina I. Kloosterman, Patricia A. Schuler, Siamak Vihidi, and Cathy E. Suroviak.
http://www.gifted.uconn.edu/nrconlin.html

Questions Parents of Gifted Students Should Ask by James Gallagher.
www.nagc.org/Publications/Parenting/question.html
Regular Classroom Practices with Gifted Students: Results of a National Survey of Classroom Teachers (1993) by Francis X. Archambault, Jr., Karen L. Westberg, Scott W. Brown, Bryan W. Hallmark, Christine L. Emmons, and Wanli Zhang
www.ucc.uconn.edu/~wwwgt/archwest.html

The following solutions were offered by the RPG. The "comments" section includes general reflections on that day's RPG meeting.

Solutions

- Have a meeting to set goals for everyone involved and to clearly set limits for when it is appropriate to set up a time to talk with the teacher.
- Ask the parent what her expectations are for her child at this age. What should he be able to do for himself?
- The teacher needs to remind herself that it is not her problem, it is the parent's problem; acknowledge that teachers have rights and if the teacher is being harassed, to involve the teachers' union to prevent further harassment.
- Perhaps this family needs family counseling and as communications open up the parent might be receptive to this suggestion by the school social worker.
- Involving the social worker in observing the child's behavior during stressful times or at the beginning of the day when the mother brings him to school might help bring documentation to support this suggestion.
- Get the child in an Affective Group dealing with friends, coping skills, peer groups, and individual advocacy skills.

Comments

We began with a discussion about how individuals felt relating to last month's discussion on being overwhelmed. Although everyone still felt the burden of too much to do and not enough time to do everything as well as they wanted, by and large they felt some relief from their stress in knowing they were not alone and that there were some strategies that, when implemented, helped.

The team of teachers and the gifted coordinator were part of this group. They felt much better about the upcoming meeting with the parent the next day. They also felt the shared anger and support of everyone there. There were some discussions about other parental problems when parents expected too much, or did not respect boundaries, or overprotected their children.

What did you learn from this case study?

CASE STUDY 6: THE EXPERIENCED TEACHER EVALUATION

Teachers may not know the district evaluation policy and expectations for evaluation. Read the following story about an experienced teacher new to the district and her first teaching evaluation.

Critical Incident

The surprise in this review was that the very things that were stated as specific strengths in her previous reviews in another school district were stated as concerns or ways her lessons did not measure up to expectations. Some of the concerns stated that her teaching was "not challenging, didn't include the grad standards, Blooms, or higher order thinking skills, her teaching didn't follow a pattern, and her goals didn't apply to what the students were doing."

These results were confusing because lesson plans, aligning goals, and teaching were such strengths in her previous district that the principal suggested she do a workshop for teachers to share her skills. Adding to the problem was the fact that the postreview conference took place several weeks after the lesson observation. The teacher had not kept a copy of the preobservation report and the principal could not find her copy.

The teacher said she had taught what she thought was a fairly typical lesson with brainstorming and cooperative learning techniques embedded and a creative emphasis to the lesson. This led to the discussion of whether or not one teaches for the kids or for the observer and the observation. If that's the case, do you match your teaching style to the administrator's style?

Other new teachers raised the issue of not knowing early on what is expected of them. Different schools and districts stress different models and these models change from year to year. Agendas can vary from building to building and principal to principal. The emerging role of graduation standards' influence on curriculum and teaching is also a question to which there seems to be mixed messages given. Then, there is the stress and anxiousness of wanting to do a good job and wanting everything to go perfectly (which it never does), and trying to rehearse a lesson (which is certainly not realistic in the day-to-day teaching) in order to get it right.

What were the surprises for the teller of this incident?

What are the beliefs about teaching and learning that help you to better understand this incident?

The evaluation policy for carrying out teacher evaluation may not reflect appropriate assessment practices. The RPG participants discussed similarities in the assessment practices for students and for teachers.

- Much that applies in evaluation and feedback for students applies in evaluation and feedback of teachers.
- Prompt and specific feedback has the most effect when wanting behavior changes.
- When there are specific criteria, clearly communicate them so that the individual knows what to do to prepare and to perform successfully.
- When expectations are confused, conflicting, or missing, the individual is left only doing what they think is expected and "right."
- The impact of evaluation on motivation is also worth consideration. If an individual has worked hard and attributes success to hard work and is found lacking, self-concept can suffer and can affect future performance negatively.
- Administrators need to keep in mind that their role as evaluator is similar to the role of the teacher evaluating students.
- It is essential to consider the effects of one's feedback on the individual receiving it.

What are solutions that you would try, given what you know about best practice and theory?

Are these solutions consistent with your beliefs about teaching and learning?

If you are interested in learning more about teacher evaluation, you may find the following resources helpful. We have included Internet links for a sampling of resources available from the Educator's Reference Desk (http://www.eduref.org).

Teacher Evaluation Policies and Practices
"Teacher evaluation systems are deemed by most school administrators and teachers to be extremely stressful, of little or no value, and a barrier to high staff morale. This report provides a review of the literature with a list of criteria and recommendations for an effective teacher evaluation process."
http://www.ssta.sk.ca/research/instruction/95-04.htm

Teacher Evaluation: New Directions & Practices
"Includes bibliography on teacher evaluation practices, related web
   resources, topical essays, forms and data for evaluation, more."
http://www.teacherevaluation.net

The Reflective Practice Groups offered the following solutions. The
"Comments" section includes general reflections on that day's RPG
meeting.

Solutions

- The teacher would be wise to talk with fellow teachers about their
  lesson plans for the next observation to get their feedback.
- The teacher should make a copy of the plan and the preobservation
  report and review them before the meeting with her supervisor.
- Schedule a follow-up meeting immediately or as soon after the observation as possible.
- Remind yourself that you are capable, that you care, that you con-
  tribute, and that one lesson observed is only a small piece of the pie.
- Talk with other teachers both before and after to have a better idea
  of what the principal is looking for or to better understand or in-
  terpret their responses.
- Make and keep a copy of your lesson plan, your preobservation re-
  port, and bring it with you to the postobservation conference.
- Ask ahead of time what the administrator is going to be looking for.
- Prepare students ahead of time.
- Request to see the observation sheet again and make some com-
  ments about your previous experiences and the timing conditions
  so that the remarks are read in that context.
- You have the right to make comments on your report.
- Ask to see the evaluation form ahead of time so that you know
  what the administrator is working from.
- Work with other teachers, the union, or your principal on develop-
  ing a rubric or a statement of criteria or standards.
- Have your mentor attend the preobservation conference with you.
- Rookies don't always know what to ask.
- Have your mentor look over the lesson and go over it with you be-

forehand. Have your mentor observe the lesson along with the principal.

- Provide release time for mentors to observe mentees before the principal does to provide coaching.
- Really put into practice the peer coaching model.
- Focus on the lesson and the kids, not on the observer.
- Make sure you pick a time that works for YOU, one that doesn't come at the same time you have a lot of other responsibilities or extra duties.
- Plant things you want the administrator to look for in the lesson plans (what you want them to be sure to notice).
- Believe in yourself.

Comments

The group decided that we should address probationary reviews since most of the new teachers had gone through or were about to go through their first one. There was a lot of discussion by everyone present regarding the changes and the impact of the grad standards on how teachers are teaching and what they think is being expected of them. This was not limited to new teachers but to everyone there. The idea of teaching to the test or teaching for the principal was something they all had trouble with, feeling that the first concern should be the kids and what is best for them.

What did you learn from this case study?

CASE STUDY 7: THE CHILD WITH NO SOCIAL SKILLS

An elementary teacher shared the following incident about a student who has been diagnosed with ADHD. The student often displays inappropriate behaviors, causing relationship problems with both peers and his teacher. The teacher labeled the incident as "Classroom Environment" because she is primarily concerned about the impact of the student's behavior on the learning environment in her classroom. The teacher shared the incident in February, when most teachers are experiencing a sense of "rejuvenation." However, clearly the teacher in this case study is not feeling "rejuvenated" by this situation.

Critical Incident

A student with inappropriate behavior problems has been diagnosed with ADHD. He has major self-esteem issues and the other kids are on his case all the time. The student is clueless. He doesn't recognize the inappropriateness of his actions. He has no social skills with other students, and engages in compulsive behaviors. His work is often not completed, he grabs things, is argumentative and controlling, ignores or doesn't read body language, and he often plays the victim. He seems to prefer negative attention.

The other students (and teachers) find him obnoxious and annoying. Students either don't want anything to do with him or get aggressive toward him. He becomes passive aggressive or pouts when the teacher attempts to discuss his behaviors with him.

In discussions with the parents, they report being frustrated at home with him as well. Even his siblings don't want to play with him.

The teacher has made a number of suggestions but there seems to be no follow-through on the part of the parents. The home seems somewhat unstable. The parents aren't introspective or reflective and don't seem to know how to follow through and don't recognize the inappropriateness of the behaviors. His parents have said they don't care about his grades or his schoolwork (and therefore don't follow through on helping make sure he does his work at home) but say they are only concerned with his making friends.

Do you agree with parents in this situation? Are they correct in focusing on their son's social behavior?

What are the beliefs about teaching and learning that help you to better understand this incident?

During the discussion of Case Study 7, the RPG participants shared the following beliefs about teaching and learning.

- The most common way for children to learn socialization skills and appropriate behavior is through observation of others (Social Learning Theory). However, in this instance, there seems to be some indication that the home may not have provided early models of appropriate behavior, so that social development is delayed.
- The child also seems to have strong attention needs that are not being met in positive ways, so he has learned that he gets attention

when he behaves inappropriately and thus this behavior is what is reinforced.

- When these patterns are learned, they are hard to change, requiring shaping and other cognitive behavioral methods to establish new patterns so that the child begins to be rewarded for appropriate behaviors and these behaviors replace the negative ones. This does require time and work and consistency and should involve the family as well, often a difficult thing to do.

What are solutions that you would try given what you know about best practice and theory?

Are these solutions consistent with your beliefs about teaching and learning?

If you would like to learn more abut the topic discussed in Case Study 7, you will find the following resources helpful. We have included Internet links for a sampling of resources available from the Educator's Reference Desk (http://www.eduref.org).

About Our Kids
"Social and Emotional Learning: What is it? How can we use it to help our children?"
http://www.aboutourkids.org/articles/socialemotional.html

ADD/ADHD: New Perspectives on Attentional Priority Disorders
"A web site with resources on inclusive learning environments for students with special needs. This website has been developed to disseminate information on successful programs, practices, and research-based strategies in Washington State. According to the site, the information at this inclusion website is in the public domain and can be freely copied and used in trainings as handouts at parent and community meetings, and in creating your school or district programs, as long as proper credit is given to the source."
http://www.newhorizons.org/spneeds/adhd/front_adhd.htm

Schoolwide and Classroom Discipline
From NWREL's School Improvement Research Series
http://www.nwrel.org/scpd/sirs/5/cu9.html

Techniques for Better Classroom Discipline
"Suggestions for achieving effective group management and control.
    There are links to additional resources at the bottom of the page."
http://www.honorlevel.com/techniques.html

The following solutions were offered by the RPG. The "comments"
section includes general reflections about that day's RPG meeting.

Solutions

- Enroll the child in a social skills group at school.
- Develop a cueing system (such as a theatrical hand signal for a cut)
  to help him become aware of when he is behaving inappropriately.
- Give him a Stop and Think reminder sheet on his desk to help him
  with his impulsivity.
- Ask the family to revisit the doctor and his medication. Some kids
  respond better to Sudafed than Ritalin.
- Have him work on skills streaming with the social worker or be
  part of a friendship–social skills group.
- Have the social worker visit the class and talk about how to help
  individuals without shouting at them.
- Discuss respect and ways of communicating respectfully.
- Have the teacher talk to the whole class to clarify roles (my job is
  to . . . your job is to . . .) and to discuss, perhaps through roleplay-
  ing, respectful and appropriate responses, a code of conduct, and
  how to interact in different classroom and playground situations.

Comments

In the course of the discussion, several teachers mentioned that they
had experienced similar kinds of situations with certain students and
how difficult this was to deal with, especially when the child was particularly annoying. They all agreed the later it gets in the year the greater
the temptation to ignore, knowing the problem will be going away as far
as they are concerned and yet it won't go away for the child.

Most agreed that the discussion provided ideas for dealing with
many of the peripheral problems that attend an annoying child (i.e.,

when classmates take over the teacher role). The teacher of the child felt that she was better prepared to deal with him and encouraged that others shared her experiences and frustrations from time to time.

What did you learn from this case study?

CASE STUDY 8: STUDENT JOURNALS AND PRIVACY ISSUES

The middle school teacher in the following incident is faced with an ethical dilemma. Does she honor student confidentiality, or not? The teacher has accurately labeled this as "Professional Responsibility." The incident was shared in late March when teachers are often leaving the "rejuvenation" stage and approaching the "reflection" stage. Just as the teacher has asked her students to reflect, so must she.

Critical Incident

As part of a course, a teacher requires students to reflect in journals. In their reflections, kids sometimes write about other teachers in ways that make it apparent who is being discussed. The teacher who requires the journals is questioning whether or not the information about other teachers, both positive and negative, should be shared with them.

Students in this class are promised anonymity and privacy for what they write in their journals. What they are saying may be important for the teachers to hear, but the students appear not to feel comfortable or safe sharing it directly with the teachers.

The teacher who requires the journals says that more than just one or two students are writing about teachers in their journals. This teacher feels that it would be possible to act as a conduit to pass the information along rather than act in an evaluative capacity. An example of the kind and level of comment being written is the following paraphrase: "Respect. In this class people don't respect the teacher or each other. I don't feel safe or like I can speak because there aren't rules."

How would you handle this situation?

The teacher might also consider this to be an "Instruction" issue. Clearly explaining the purpose of the assignment and the type of feedback that will be provided might greatly alleviate the ethical dilemma associated with this critical incident. Also, viewing the feedback as instructional can move this incident in a different direction.

What are the beliefs about teaching and learning that help you to better understand this incident?

During the discussion of Case Study 8, the RPG participants shared the following beliefs about teaching and learning.

- Schools have particular channels for evaluation and feedback to teachers. These channels are generally hierarchical and well defined and usually do not include students.
- Teachers relate as colleagues. That relationship can be upset when a teacher steps out of the nonevaluative mode, even if it is just to pass along information.
- Evaluation/Criticism are seen as an inherent part of that kind of exchange.

What are solutions that you would try given what you know about best practice and theory?

Are these solutions consistent with your beliefs about teaching and learning?

If you would like to learn more abut the topic discussed in Case Study 8, you will find the following resources helpful. We have included Internet links for a sampling of resources available from the Educator's Reference Desk (http://www.eduref.org).

Journal Writing Everyday: Teachers Say It Really Works by Gary Hopkins
"Education World talked with teachers who use daily journal writing in their classrooms." This article also includes a thread for teachers to post ideas for writing prompts that work with their students.
http://www.education-world.com/a_curr/curr144.shtml

ERIC Digest - Writing Instruction: Current Practices in the Classroom (2000)
http://www.ericfacility.net/ericdigests/ed446338.html

The following solutions were offered by the RPG. The "comments" section includes general reflections on that day's RPG meeting.

Solutions

- Decide not to share the information on the basis that the message isn't wanted from the messenger and, therefore, the messenger becomes the loser.
- Work to build in systemic means for gaining student feedback on a regular basis.

Comments

What message gets delivered when someone speaks for someone else—when you do not keep it direct? Within the system as it stands, who can legitimately give teachers feedback and offer criticism? Would this issue be laid out the same way in the middle school and/or elementary school setting? How do the dynamics among staff differ in different schools within the district? Why? What would have to change systemically and philosophically for students to feel like they can give feedback more directly? More basic even, is student feedback credible? Once received, are teachers allowed to decide that negative feedback is inaccurate and continue as before because what they are doing makes sense in the long run? Or does all student feedback need to result in teacher change?

What did you learn from this case study?

CASE STUDY 9: GRADE-LEVEL MEETING WITH SPECIAL EDUCATION TEAM AND PRINCIPAL

The special education teacher in the following incident is faced with a common dilemma—what is her role in an inclusive classroom? She has labeled this incident as "Professional Responsibility." The incident was shared in late March when teachers are often leaving the "rejuvenation" stage and approaching the "reflection" stage.

Critical Incident

People involved: Special Education Teachers #1 (teller), #2, and #3, first grade teachers, and the building principal. Last Tuesday, Teacher #1 had another meeting and was not able to attend the meeting with Teachers #2 and 3 and the building principal during which the teachers reported that they had completed 22 special education assessments during the year and Teacher #1 had only completed four assessments. Teachers 2 and 3 felt that it was unfair that Teacher #1 had completed so few. In the schedule, Teacher #1 had built in 20 minutes a day for assessments. The other two teachers had built in an average of over an hour a day for assessments.The first grade teacher present said that sometimes you (a teacher) get more kids that need help than others. That can't be predicted. Teacher #1 has been regularly teaching a reading group in each first grade classroom. The others decided that she wouldn't do two of the reading groups to free up more time for assessments. The first grade teacher added that there are seldom special education students identified in first grade.

Teacher #1's involvement in regular classes helps to assess the children's performance on a daily basis. Although students aren't formally identified, she knows that some of them will be eventually, and at least she can provide service now using an inclusive model. If Teacher #1 did stop doing two reading groups, the 20-minute slots would not be together, thus of little value in assessment time. The first grade teachers want to sit down with all three special education teachers. The other two special education teachers need to be flexible in order to carry out the ideas for inclusion.

Conflicts between faculty members can be particularly unpleasant and difficult to manage. What are the beliefs about teaching and learning that help you to better understand this incident?

During the discussion of Case Study 9, the RPG participants shared the following beliefs about teaching and learning:

- Children that are identified as needing Special Education services do not always get them in Inclusive Classrooms.
- If Inclusion is going to work, the Special Education Teachers and Regular Education Teachers all have to work together and be flexible.
- Children in first grade benefit by having a Special Education teacher as a regular part of their classroom. She can assess their needs and provide support and also give information to the classroom teacher.
- One bonus for Inclusion is less testing/labeling down the line.
- Problems can be helped early.

- Special Education teachers should not determine fairness of work-load by counting the number of assessments that they complete.
- Focus on the learner: In the Inclusive Classroom are some identi-fied children receiving the amount of services that they need? Are some students falling through the cracks?
- Kids who don't qualify for Chapter I/Title I receive services any-way because of the Special Education teacher being a regular part of the classroom.

What are solutions that you would try given what you know about best practice and theory?

Are these solutions consistent with your beliefs about teaching and learning?

If you would like to learn more about the topic discussed in Case Study 9, you will find the following resources helpful. We have included Internet links for a sampling of resources available from the Educator's Reference Desk (http://www.eduref.org).

Inclusive Learning Environments for Students with Special Learning Needs

"A web site with resources on inclusive learning environments for students with special needs. This website has been developed to disseminate information on successful programs, practices, and research-based strategies in Washington State. According to the site, the information at this inclusion website is in the public do-main and can be freely copied and used in trainings as handouts at parent and community meetings, and in creating your school or district programs, as long as proper credit is given to the source." http://www.newhorizons.org/spneeds/inclusion/front_inclusion.htm

Early Childhood research Institute on Inclusion (ECRII) (August 2000).

"The ECRII was a five-year national research project funded by the Office of Special Education Programs, U.S. Department of Edu-cation. The ECRII studies the inclusion of preschool children with disabilities in typical preschool, day care and community settings. http://www.fpg.unc.edu/~ecrii/

Co-Teaching: Are Two Heads Better Than One in an Inclusive Class-room? By Millicent Lawton Harvard Education Letter Research on Line.
www.edletter.org/past/issues/1999-ma/coteaching.shtml

The following solutions were offered by the RPG. The "comments" section includes general reflections on that day's RPG meeting.

Solutions

- Teacher #1 wracked her brain to find solutions that would provide her with more time for assessments, even though we do not have kids that currently need to be assessed. Now the building principal said that she would hire a paraprofessional to take the two reading groups.
- Teacher #1 feels bad because she is being ousted from an experience she thinks is making a difference to first graders.
- Could the money from Learning Readiness be used?
- Teacher #1 has children in reading groups after they completed paper work. The building principal said that if people requested that again it would have to come through the teachers' union.
- Is there a policy for prep time for teachers of special education?

What did you learn from this case study?

CASE STUDY 10: HOW MUCH IS ENOUGH?

The teacher in the following incident is doing the balancing act—trying to determine where she should focus her energies. She has labeled this incident as "Professional Responsibility." The incident was shared in April when many teachers are in the "reflection" stage. As the current school year is coming to a close, teachers tend to reflect on their role in the larger scheme of the school experience.

Critical Incident

The teachers have just had a week's break and already feel the stresses of too much to do. There are the second evaluation observations to be scheduled and endured, proxy tests, professional competence tests, action research, Assurance of Mastery evaluations due, portfolios due, summer school planning and meetings, staff and staffing meetings, meetings with parents, students, mentor-mentee conferences, curriculum meetings, special education meetings, P.T.O., school special events, and meetings regarding the transferring of students due to boundary changes.

This last set of meetings has additional stresses because of the media pressure and the feeling that they are expected to "sell their school." This boundary change has resulted in open informational meetings scheduled for parents with the expectation that teachers will be there. At this point it feels like there have been no conversations regarding how the changes should occur, what approach should be taken, and what should be done.

The teachers see it as a district decision, and a district problem, with the expectation that the school and the teachers will handle meeting deadlines and quotas without knowing who is coming. In addition to these issues are the related timing issues surrounding special education assessment when there is a sudden increase in enrollment and what that does to the scheduling of ongoing cases.

Then there is the scheduling of district and state tests that seem to hit some grades with greater frequency than others and involve multiple days of testing during which regular curriculum needs to take a back seat.

It's hard to meet all the demands of meetings and deadlines and still develop and teach with enthusiasm the appropriate curriculum teachers are hired to teach. Most teachers would love to have time to spend on curriculum planning, teaching, and working with their kids and have all the other demands disappear. There just doesn't seem to be enough time and energy to do all that is required in a 24-hour day!

At times, all teachers have feelings similar to those expressed in Case Study 10. What are the beliefs about teaching and learning that help you to better understand this incident?

During the discussion of Case Study 10, the RPG participants shared the following beliefs about teaching and learning.

Theories Behind Practice

It is possible to apply Glasser's Control Theory of basic needs to this situation. As Glasser defines the five basic needs, they are Belonging (other people, your team, your family), Freedom (choice, control, What can I do? What can I let go of?), Power (accomplishment, self worth), Fun (humor, joy), and Survival (basic needs of health, food, safety, shelter). According to Reality Therapy it is important to keep these in balance.

When looking at the above sense of being overwhelmed, powerless, and unable to feel like you are accomplishing anything, feeling as though you have no control over the circumstances, not to mention having time for yourself or fun, it is easy to see why teachers feel frustrated and fear burning out. It is wise to take into consideration meeting these needs in the workplace for teachers as well as for students.

What are solutions that you would try given what you know about best practice and theory?

Are these solutions consistent with your beliefs about teaching and learning?

If you would like to learn more about the topic discussed in Case Study 10, you will find the following resources helpful. We have included Internet links for a sampling of resources available from the Educator's Reference Desk (http://www.eduref.org).

New-teacher Excellence: Retaining Our Best (December 2002)
"In this report from the Alliance for Excellent Education, the authors 'examine what we know about effective induction programs and offer examples of programs around the nation that might serve as models for others.'"
http://www.all4ed.org/publications/NewTeacherExcellence/NTE.pdf

What to Expect Your First Year of Teaching (September 1998)
"Based on discussions among winners of the 1996 First Class Teacher Awards, this document contains advice for new teachers, those who educate teachers, and others interested. Questions asked of the participants included: What was it like the first year? What were your toughest challenges, your greatest rewards? Did you get the right preparation? Do you have any insights you could offer new teachers?"
http://www.ed.gov/pubs/FirstYear

The following solutions were offered by the RPG. The "comments" section includes general reflections on that day's RPG meeting:

- Stop, take a deep breath.
- Play Mozart in the car, in the classroom.
- Dim the lights.
- Find the humor in the situation.
- Laugh about things with friends and colleagues.
- Exercise, walk the dog.
- Just say "No."
- Decide what is most important and tackle that.
- Don't agree to take on anything new unless you give up something.
- Decide your priorities and let the rest go.
- More isn't better.
- Be well planned and organized.
- Don't be afraid to change the things that need changing that you have power to change.
- Don't be afraid to leave some things out; you don't have to put everything in.
- Communicate!
- Share.
- Ask for help.

Comments

Teachers felt good about being a part of this group even though it was another meeting. They commented on the shared wisdom and the sense that they were not alone and that the group managed to find humor and laugh at the same time that problems were being shared.

What did you learn from this case study?

Epilogue

Retention of "highly qualified" teachers is a national concern. According to newly released data from the National Commission on Teaching and America's Future, about 30 percent of the nation's teaching force is either leaving the profession or entering the profession each year.[1] Therefore, it is imperative that an ongoing program of support and encouragement be provided to our teachers. Although originally designed for new teachers, we have found that Reflective Practice Groups (RPGs) are effective with novice and experienced teachers in urban and suburban schools, charter schools, and with preservice teachers. The emphasis on collegial conversation, nonevaluative analysis, and reflective thinking make RPGs an excellent vehicle for faculty support and development. One need only listen to the words of RPG participants to be convinced of their value:

> "I am certain I am making a difference in the lives of my students!"
>
> "I have become more empathetic to other teachers—more able to look outside myself and therefore have become a better team member."
>
> "When a person is happy and feeling positive about their job and colleagues (support, warmth) they are able to really concentrate on their jobs and students."

Certainly this high degree of efficacy is what we would hope for all teachers!

NOTES

1. National Commission on Teaching and America's Future, 2000.

The Reflective Practice Group Process

The Reflective Practice Group Process

Convene the group

- Establish rules for how the group will function
- Discuss confidentiality

1. Each person writes down a critical incident that s/he has experienced since the last meeting. Give the incident one of the following labels: Planning and Preparation, Classroom Environment, Instruction, or Professional Responsibilities.
2. Each person briefly shares his/her incident with the group. No embellishments or questions at this point.
3. The group chooses one of the shared incidents to discuss more fully.
4. The group asks the teller of the incident for more details—clarifying information, impact on others, teacher's feelings about the incident.
5. Each person writes down answers to the following questions: What are the beliefs about teaching and learning that help us to better understand this incident? Why was this an effective or ineffective approach?
6. Each person shares his/her responses to #5.
7. The group engages in a discussion of the following: What can you learn from this incident that will help you in future situations? Is the action you would take consistent with the image that you want to project of who you are as a teacher?
8. The group facilitator summarizes the discussion.

Reflective Practice Group Worksheet

Critical Incident:

Choose a label for your incident: Planning and Preparation
                                Classroom Environment
                                Instruction
                                Professional Responsibilities

What are the beliefs about teaching and learning that help you to better understand this incident?

What can you learn from this incident that will help you in future situations? Is the action you would take consistent with the image that you want to project as a teacher?

Notes:

Bibliography

Britzman, Deborah P. 1991. *Practice Makes Practice: A Critical Study of Learning to Teach.* Albany: State University of New York Press.

Brookfield, Stephen, D. 1995. *Becoming a Critically Reflective Teacher.* San Francisco: Jossey-Bass.

Cady, Joan M., Linda Schaak Distad, and Richard Germundsen. 1998. "Reflective Practice Groups in Teacher Induction: Building Professional Community Via Experiential Knowledge." *Education* 118: 459–70.

Center for Instructional Development and Research. 2002. *Talking with Colleagues about Teaching—Resources and Examples.* (http://depts.Washington.edu/cidrweb/conversations.html)

Chase, Betsy, Richard Germundsen, Joan Cady Brownstein, and Linda Distad. 2001. "Making the Connection between Increased Student Learning and Reflective Practice." *Educational Horizons* 79: 143–47.

Danielson, Charlotte. 1996. *Enhancing Professional Practice: A Framework for Teachers.* Alexandria, Virginia: Association for Supervision and Curriculum Development.

Dewey, John. 1910/1997. *How We Think.* New York: Dover Publications.

Distad, Linda and Joan Cady Brownstein. *Reflective Practice Groups* (http://minerva.stkate.edu/academic/educases.nsp).

Distad, Linda, Schaak, Betsy Chase, Richard Germundsen, and Joan Cady Brownstein. 2000. "Putting Their Heads Together." *Journal of Staff Development* 21: 49–51.

Educational Testing Services. *Praxis III: Classroom Performance Assessments* (www.ets.org).

Even, M. 1987. Why Adults Learn in Different Ways. *Lifelong Learning: An Omnibus of Practice and Research* 57: 22–25, 27.

Hiebert, James, Robert Gallimore, and James W. Stigler. 2002. "A Knowledge Base for the Teaching Profession: What It Looks Like, and How Can We Get One?" *Educational Researcher* 31: 3–15.

Interstate New Teacher Assessment and Support Consortium. *Model Standards for Beginning Teacher Licensing and Development: A Resource for State Dialogue.* (www.ccso/content/pdfs/corestrd.pdf).

Jackson, Philip W. 1990. *Life in Classrooms.* New York: Teachers College Press, Columbia University.

Lambert, Linda. 1995. "Toward a Theory of Constructivist Leadership." In Linda Lambert, Deborah Walker, Diane P. Zimmerman, Joanne E. Cooper, Morgan Dale Lambert, Mary E. Gardner, and P. J. Ford Slack, eds., *The Constructivist Leader.* New York: Teachers College Press, Columbia University.

———. 1998. *Building Leadership Capacity in Schools.* Alexandria, Va.: Association for Supervision and Curriculum Development.

Model Standards for Beginning Teacher Licensing and Development: A Resource for State Dialogue. (www.ccso.org/intasc.html)

Moir, E., and C. Stubbe. 1995. "Professional Growth for New Teachers: Support and Assessment through Collegial Partnership." *Teacher Education Quarterly* 22 (fall): 83–91.

National Board for Professional Teaching Standards. (www.nbpts.org/strds.ofm).

National Commission on Teaching and America's Future. 2003. *No Dream Denied: A Pledge to America's Children* (www.ndtaf.org/dream/dread.html)

Palmer, Parker J. 1998. *The Courage to Teach: Exploring the Inner Landscape of a Teacher's Life.* San Francisco: Jossey-Bass.

A Project of the Institute on Disability, UAP, University of New Hampshire. 2002. *Teaching and Learning Tools: What is Reflective Practice.* (http://iod.unh.edu/EE/archive-relfective.html).

Schön, Donald. 1983. *The Reflective Practitioner: How Professionals Think in Action.* New York: Basic Books.

Smyth, John. 1989. *Critical Perspectives on Educational Leadership.* London: Falmer Press.

Stansbury, Kendyll, and Joy Zimmerman. 2000. *Lifelines to the Classroom: Designing Support for Beginning Teachers.* San Francisco: WestEd.

Tanner, Laurel. 2000. *Dewey's Laboratory School: Lessons for Today.* New York: Teachers College Press, Columbia University.

Vera, G. R. 1998. *Methodologias de Investigacion Docente: La Investigacion Protagonica. Santiago, Chile: Programa Interdisciplinario de Investigacion en Educacion.*

York-Barr, Jennifer, William A. Sommers, Gail S. Ghere, and Jo Montie. 2001. *Reflective Practice to Improve Schools.* Thousand Oaks, Calif.: Corwin Press.

Index

About the Authors

Linda Schaak Distad is currently associate dean for education programs at the College of St. Catherine in St. Paul, Minnesota. Dr. Distad has been an educator for over thirty years, having taught at both the elementary school level and in higher education.

Dr. Joan Cady Brownstein has been an educator for thirty-five years in Minnesota and Pennsylvania, with teaching experience in K-12 vocal music, elementary education, and teacher education. Currently Dr. Brownstein is associate professor in the School of Education, University of St. Thomas, Minnesota.